FEMINISM AND LINGUISTIC THEORY

FEMINISM AND LINGUISTIC THEORY

Deborah Cameron

MACMILLAN

First published 1985 by
THE MACMILLAN PRESS LTD
London and Basingstoke
Companies and representatives
throughout the world

Printed in Hong Kong

British Library Cataloguing in Publication Data
Cameron, Deborah
Feminism and linguistic theory
1. Woman and language
I. Title
400   P120.W6
ISBN 0-333-37077-5
ISBN 0-333-37078-3 Pbk

Contents

Preface: On Demystification

As a feminist academic, I am aware of certain obligations and responsibilities. I am conscious, for instance, that many women have been denied the privilege of higher education. By this I certainly don't mean the chance to imbibe 'wisdom' from 'great minds', nor even the opportunity to develop and discuss ideas, which feminists do anyway. I mean the right to financial support, the right to organise your own time, and the right to use the informational, technical, social and recreational facilities of a college or university. In our society these are privileges indeed, and women get less of a share in them than men.

I also realise that many women consider higher education the very reverse of a privilege. They are only too delighted never to have sold their souls and brains to the repressive patriarchal values of academic institutions.

So my responsibilities are these. First, I must be responsive to the needs and concerns of women outside academic life; and secondly I must challenge the practices and values that keep women outside.

Because of these obligations, I have tried to write this book in a particular way, one that I feel embodies feminist principles. That in itself is a challenge to the status quo; and the essence of the challenge lies in my concern to demystify language and linguistics.

Intellectual mystification occurs when a writer, to put herself in a position of authority, denies the reader sufficient resources to understand and dispute what she says. It can be done in a number of ways.

For example, the writer may leave unexplained and taken for granted the conceptual framework she is working in, or may present it as a given rather than something open to question. Or she may depersonalise herself, hiding behind the spurious authority of an 'objective commentator' by not making it clear where she stands, politically and intellectually, in relation to the ideas she discusses.

In this book, therefore, I have tried to spell out even the most basic assumptions behind the theories I deal with, and to provide enough background to suggest how they may be called into question themselves. I have been at pains to make clear what my own opinions are, and to present the opinions of others scrupulously. To do this I have used a lot of quotation – which allows my subjects to some extent to speak for themselves – and it is important that the reader scrutinise that quotation carefully.

Another important source of mystification in academic writings is the language used: indeed, it could be said that mystification BY language and mystification OF language are the joint subjects of this book. Writers may prevent readers from dealing with their ideas as anything more than gibberish, or as anything less than received truth, by writing in a way that is incomprehensible. Alternatively, they may be so vague that no clear line of thought emerges. Then, if they are criticised, it is easy for them to claim they have been misinterpreted.

In this book I have attempted a relatively simple style. An important addition to the text is the glossary of linguistic and other technical terms, which the reader should refer to whenever necessary for a concise account of what I mean by using various unfamiliar words.

I have avoided language that conceals the presence of the writer and the process of writing. The word *I* appears frequently, and at many points I indicate exactly what argument I am trying to put forward. The aim here is to give the reader every opportunity of saying to herself, 'hold on a minute, that doesn't follow', or 'but what about x?' or 'I can't accept that'. In other words, the reader is encouraged to be an active maker of her own ideas in relation to this book, and not simply a passive consumer of other people's.

I have also avoided offensive and sexist language, replacing it either with 'neutral' terminology or, more often, with terms that draw attention to the existence of women. Most sex-indefinite and generic referents in this book will be *she* and *her*. If there are any men reading who feel uneasy about being excluded, or not addressed, they may care to consider that women get this feeling within minutes of opening the vast majority of books, and to reflect on the effect it has.

Finally, I acknowledge that I did not write this book unaided: many groups and individuals contributed to it in different ways. Some of them participated in discussions of language and sex; some showed me their work, or shared information and experiences they thought might be useful; some read and commented on the typescript; some gave me encouragement and support while I was writing it. One particular group, my students, helped me by obliging me to concentrate on the basics of linguistic theory and to work out the best ways of explaining them.

I would like to thank the following in particular: participants in the first WAVAW conference workshop on language and violence; members of Balliol College Women's Group, Pembroke College Women's Group, Oxford University Women in Politics seminar and Oxford Rape Crisis Group; Kate Cameron, Tony Crowley, Liz Frazer, Ian Griffiths, Roy Harris, Caroline Henton, Rebecca Hiscock, Radhika Holmström, Bob Hoyle, Helen Lawrence, Toril Moi, Peter Mühlhäusler, M. Nawaz, Elizabeth Powell-Jones and Marni Stanley.

D.C.

1 Introduction: Language and Feminism

> We have inherited a
> contaminated language....
>
> *Mary Daly*
>
> ...how can we conceive of a
> revolutionary struggle which
> does not involve a revolution
> in discourse?
>
> *Julia Kristeva*

The question of language and its political implications has exercised writers, philosophers and social theorists throughout the intellectual history of western civilisation. It is noticeable, too, that the subject has inspired extreme pessimism: from ancient Greece to Orwell's *Nineteen Eighty-Four*, speech and writing have been credited with a malign power to regulate human social relations in ways we are not aware of, and to disguise abstract truths in a cloud of misleading rhetoric.

Today's speakers inherit the view that language is a weapon, used by the powerful to oppress their subordinates. But why should language, and knowledge about the workings of language, be a resource for the powerful alone? Why shouldn't the weapons of reaction be appropriated by the other side?

Mary Daly and Julia Kristeva are among the women who have argued in their writings for a radical theory of language, not as an intellectual luxury, but as an essential part of the struggle for women's liberation. In the last few years it seems their voices have been heard, and problems of language and linguistic analysis have entered the arena of feminist debate. Women have begun to talk about words, and to change them. In this book, then, I am making a contribution not only to an ancient tradition but also to feminist work in progress.

But why add another book to the pile? A number of books and

1

a host of articles are available to feminists already. What do I hope to contribute? It is true that feminist awareness of language as an issue has never been greater, and that a good deal has been published on the subject. Yet in this accumulating literature there is a diversity of approach and viewpoint which I find something of a problem. What common ground is there between, say, the sociolinguist's statistical analyses of sex difference (e.g. Philip Smith),[1] the reformists' prescriptions for eliminating sexism in everyday usage (e.g. Casey Miller and Kate Swift),[2] and the radical call for a revolution in language which will liberate us all? Are they addressing the same question? What questions should they be addressing? If their conclusions differ, are they all equally valid? What, in short, is the state of the art? This is what I set out to assess.

I have other reasons for writing. First, to supplement the available material by bringing the different approaches I have mentioned together in a spirit of critical examination. My aim is to explain ideas about language clearly, and with enough background theoretical discussion for readers to decide for themselves what is correct and what is open to question.

My second motive is that I have never encountered opinions similar to mine in feminist writings on language. As I am an active feminist who also happens to be a linguist, it has been exciting for me to see the growth of interest in language that has recently occurred in the women's movement: but I am sorry the movement seems to be adopting an orthodoxy on the subject which is rarely challenged, and with which I disagree.

Finally, I want to attempt in this book a critique of academic linguistics. This is not just a matter of pointing out sexist assumptions and practices, important though that may be: more radically, it involves questioning the whole scientific/objective basis of linguistics, and showing how the practices of linguists are implicated in patriarchal ideology and oppression.

Before I explore any of these points further, however, I want to consider why feminists should take an interest in language at all, and to talk about the forms their interest has taken in the past. It is often said that the most distinctively human quality we possess is the ability to communicate with each other by means of languages, and that linguistic communication is crucial to the organisation of human societies. So people with an interest in the workings of any society must also concern themselves with its language – how it is structured and used, what its users believe about it and so on. These are, broadly speaking, the questions linguistic theory is supposed to deal with.

Feminists are deeply interested in the workings of their societies, since in order to fight their oppression they must first understand it. Much feminist effort is directed, therefore, to reanalysing society as a patriarchy, a system in which men have power over women. Language is part of patriarchy. If it plays a crucial part in social organisation it is instrumental in maintaining male power, and feminists must study its workings carefully.

So it is not entirely astonishing that the last few years have seen a noticeable upsurge of interest in language, affecting not only academics but women throughout the women's movement. You can see this upsurge, for instance, in the fact that many women's conferences on subjects ranging from violence to trades unionism now include a workshop or a paper on language. A few years ago, this would have seemed a very esoteric subject for grass-roots feminism: yet at the first WAVAW conference in 1981, I was struck by the intensity with which language was discussed. The women present had evidently given it a lot of thought, and were emphatic on the need to include language in their political analyses. They were very aware of their own usage, and many were making conscious efforts to change it.

In the last two years, too, I have heard of women and language groups being set up and producing material; noted the proliferation of sections on language in women's studies texts; watched the subject of language and sex appear in lecture courses, exam questions and research proposals at Oxford University; and read with interest a number of new books on language, produced by feminists for a feminist readership. The best known of these, Dale Spender's *Man Made Language*, received enough media coverage to put the subject of women and language on the map for many people outside the women's movement.

All this indicates that in language, feminists have pinpointed a major theoretical and practical issue. But how and why has it emerged? Although it has recently taken new forms and acquired a new importance, interest in language among feminists is not a new phenomenon. Language used to be discussed, in the early years of 'second wave' feminist activity, under the general heading of 'representation'.

This term embraced not only the language used about women,

but also the way they were in general depicted by the mass media. Particular attention was paid to genres thought especially likely to inculcate or reinforce sexism, such as school textbooks, children's fiction and advertising. On the simple assumption that people's attitudes will be affected by something they see repeatedly, feminists exposed, and tried to eliminate, negative and stereotypical portrayals of women.

Where language was concerned, the representation lobby advocated 'non-sexist writing'. A usage was in need of reform if it was either blatantly offensive ('Blonde in fatal car-crash'; 'Bitches wear furs') or androcentric, implying that the norm of humanity is male ('Man', 'Mankind', 'Man in the street', etc.) Reform consisted of recasting expressions to make them neutral (so 'mankind' becomes 'humanity', 'man in the street' becomes 'average person' and so on). This was supposed magically to bring women into our mental landscapes. As early as 1973 a major publisher, McGraw-Hill, circulated its authors with guidelines on non-sexist writing.

Recently, however, a new kind of conern with language has become more common among feminists, and the new theorists warn that non-sexist language is an illusion. They stress that language is pervaded by sexism, and that women are alienated from it because it is controlled by men.

Some linguistic scholars would like to dismiss this development as mere academic fashion. We are currently in a period of great concern among progressive intellectuals about language. These thinkers, working in areas like literary and film criticism, psychoanalysis and cultural theory, are often called 'structuralists' or 'semiologists' because of their debt to the linguist Saussure. They centre their analyses on language, believing that human culture is characterised by the creation of languages (discourses) which structure our view of the world.

Feminism is an important current in this sort of work. However, it is only recently that British feminists outside the academic world have become interested in it. Although Dale Spender, for example, has read semiological writers like Luce Irigaray and Cora Kaplan, both she and her audience are more at home in the Anglo-American tradition of linguistics and anthropology. The resurgence of interest we are discussing may have brought semiology to the notice of a wider audience, but it is not the consequence of the current vogue for structuralism.

Nor can we attribute it simply to the writings of Dale Spender and her colleagues (many of whom wrote in comparative obscurity for some time before her). The publicity fanfare with which *Man Made Language* was greeted showed this was an idea whose time had come. Suddenly, it seemed, feminists wanted to think and read about language. Why? It could be argued that forces within feminism itself make women aware of language and its problems. This is because the use of language is at the heart of feminist political practice.

Nowhere is this centrality clearer than in the practice of consciousness-raising (CR), where women uncover the roots and the precise nature of their oppression by talking to each other about their experience. Often, women who have spent time in CR groups emphasise how liberating it is to be able to put into words experiences which had seemed nebulous, so private and personal as to be unmentionable; and to find these experiences are understood and shared by other women.

Many feminist writers have referred to this communication of shared experience as *naming*, but in fact a name, a label, is not always necessary. Sometimes one is coined – *sexism*, for instance, which handily encapsulates a whole area of women's experience – but at other times it is enough to define an experience by describing it and getting others to acknowledge it. There is still no name for Betty Friedan's 'problem without a name', but we all now know what it is.[3] Language has dispelled its air of non-existence not by naming it but by communicating it.

The need to communicate, to bridge the gap between women, is a constant theme of feminist writing, reflected very often in the titles of books and poems (*Silences; Lies, Secrets and Silence; Dream of a Common Language; Finding a Voice; Unlearning To Not Speak*). Silence is a symbol of oppression, while liberation is speaking out, making contact. The contact is what matters; a woman who lies or who is silent may not lack a language, but she does not communicate.

Women struggling to reinterpret their experience have noticed again and again that language itself does not guarantee communication, and many feel actually inhibited by the inadequacy of words. A woman writes:

Sometimes when I am talking to people I really feel at a loss for words. I have this idea in my head and a feeling I want to

express, and I just can't get it out. I have felt like this for years
and I have never been able to understand why.... A vast
number of the words I use all the time to describe my
experience are not really describing it at all.[4]

What this woman is describing has been called women's
'alienation' from language. It is an uneasy feeling that your words
are not yours at all – they have been somehow co-opted, or taken
away and turned against you. The feminist view of language is
reminiscent of the feminist view of sexuality: it is a powerful
resource which the oppressor has appropriated, giving back only
the shadow which women need to function in patriarchal society.
From this point of view, reclaiming women's language is indeed
crucial for women's liberation.

Some writers try to reclaim language by making its inad-
equacies visible in wordplay. Many semiologists favour this
approach, and it is used by Mary Daly in her classic text
Gyn/Ecology. Daly wants us to look behind the taken-for-granted
senses of words, so she restructures them; *re-member, crone-
logical, the/rapist, a-maze*.[5] But while this strategy exposes the
deceptiveness of words by confronting the reader with the extent
to which she normally fails to question them, it does not explain
why language presents this problem, nor suggest any solution.
This is one more incentive for women to look towards a
comprehensive feminist theory of language.

Impelled, then, not only by outside influences but more
importantly by feminist practice itself, feminists have begun to
develop a linguistic theory. They have started to explore the
disciplines which look useful, particularly sociolinguistics (the
study of language and society, how social differences interact with
linguistic ones and what the role of language in culture is) and
semiology, which among other things tries to explain how
children develop 'gendered subjectivity' (i.e. a sense of themselves
as men or women in their society) in terms of a sex-differentiated
relation to language.

Three areas of investigation have been identified by
proponents of feminist language theory. First, there is the study
of sex-difference; do men and women use language differently,
and if so, what does this mean? Secondly, there is sexism in
language, its effects, and how to eliminate it. And thirdly, there

is alienation: is this 'the oppressor's language', within which we cannot articulate our experience as women?

In all of these areas, work has been done: in all of them, much remains to be done. One of the most important outstanding problems is to clarify our underlying theory of the relation between language and world view. Like a wolf-whistle, a sexist remark has a significance above and beyond the immediate offence it gives: it is the outward manifestation of an unacceptable misogyny. But is it also, as many feminists believe, the very mechanism by which misogyny is constructed and transmitted? Can we think outside the confines of a woman-hating language?

It is here, and at similar points where general theoretical matters are at issue, that feminists have much to gain by turning to linguistic theory, provided they understand, and have some way of assessing, conflicting views. An additional hazard they face is the sexism which affects linguistics as it does other academic disciplines; again, it is necessary to understand the nature of argument, methodology, etc. in linguistics before you can tell how much of it is pure moonshine.

Many women feel incapable of making this sort of judgement. I have often heard feminists complain that the theories underlying much of the work on language mystify them, and they do not know whether to accept what they read. Often they are interested in the broad questions feminist work on language raises, and would like more background information; but they do not know where to find it.

This book is addressed to those women. In it they will find an introduction to the most influential relevant trends in linguistic theory (Chapters 1 and 2); a critique of sex difference studies (Chapter 3); an account of sexism in grammar and in language, with a discussion of possible reform strategies (Chapters 4 and 5); a detailed consideration of the language-and-world view question, with an account of several radical linguistic theories (Chapters 6 and 7); an alternative theory based on a communicational approach (Chapter 8) and a conclusion (Chapter 9) which looks at the prospects for an adequate feminist theory of language, as well as for a feminist linguistic practice.

It is inevitable that the feminist debate about language – what it means and what we should be doing about it – will become ever more complex and difficult for the non-specialist to evaluate: the major challenge is to keep the discussion accessible without blinking difficult theoretical problems. In this book I have tried to meet that challenge.

2 Linguistic Theory: Frameworks and Approaches

> ...the study of language has opened
> the route to an understanding of
> mankind [sic], social history and
> the laws of how a society functions.
>
> *Rosalind Coward and John Ellis*

I have already mentioned the three areas which a feminist theory of language must deal with: sex differences, sexism and the question of alienation. In saying this I am not saying anything new. Although as far as I know, no one has ever put out a manifesto for feminist language study aiming to define the subject matter comprehensively, history and consensus dictate that these things should be the proper focus for our efforts.

As well as charting the terrain, albeit informally, feminists have begun to explore it. In their researches they have drawn mainly on two disciplines: modern linguistics and contemporary semiology. The most popular texts, and those read in departments of linguistics, tend to the approach known as *socio-linguistics*, a branch of (predominantly Anglo-American) linguistic science; but there is also a considerable body of work by feminists whose allegiance is to semiology (represented in Britain by journals such as *m/f* and *Screen*, and in America by *Signs* and *Diacritics*: in France they are more numerous, and a good introductory anthology is that by E. Marks and I. de Courtivron).[1]

In this book I intend to develop and to criticise both of these approaches, in themselves and as they relate to feminism. It is therefore important that the reader should have some basic understanding of linguistics and semiology from the start; and this chapter is devoted to explaining the basic principles of linguistic and semiological theory.

WHAT IS LINGUISTICS?

The usual definition of linguistics simply calls it 'the scientific study of language'. *Scientific* is the important word here: for although language has been studied for at least 2500 years in the guise of grammar (how to use language correctly), rhetoric (how to use it persuasively), poetics (literary criticism) and philology (historical analysis and comparison of different languages), the scientific study of language is a specifically modern development. Most introductory textbooks date it from the publication in 1916 of Ferdinand de Saussure's *Cours de Linguistique Générale* (Course in General Linguistics).

Before we turn to Saussure, or consider what it means in general to say that the study of language can be scientific, it is important to examine what it means to call any kind of enquiry 'scientific'.

The dictionary definition of *science* is 'a branch of knowledge dealing with objects, forces and phenomena of the natural universe, based on systematic observation of facts and seeking to formulate general explanatory laws'. Evidently this description in its entirety will only do for the 'natural' sciences like physics and chemistry. Other subjects usually thought of as scientific, such as computing science and psychology, do not deal with 'objects, forces and phenomena of the natural universe' (and neither does linguistics.) But we can make these less immediately concrete areas of enquiry as much like the prestigious natural sciences as possible by extending to them the most important connotations of *science*.

According to these connotations, science is *factual* – it deals with fact, not wild guesses or opinions. Thus the scientist has to be *objective* and *methodical*, rather than biased, casual, haphazard or anything else that might interfere with the facts. Finally, scientists are obliged to provide not only facts but *explanations*, by discovering the laws of how things work: which implies that anything a scientist studies must have laws for her to find, rather than operating at random.

The other, very important, connotation of science is its high value and prestige. Science, in the imagination of scientists and non-scientists alike, is good. The qualities it is thought to have may in fact be complete myths (objectivity, for instance; and many non-scientific qualities like intuition and guesswork actually play a significant part in all investigations) but the mythology of science is one that our culture worships. We believe that science, distinguished from the arts by its objectivity and from scholarship (e.g. history) by its power to explain things, will lead us to the truth.

So when we examine the development of a scientific linguistics we must bear in mind that there is a great deal to be gained, in terms of credibility and respect, from the use of the label *scientific*. In linguistics, as in other disciplines, deliberate attempts have been made to appear as objective, rigorous, etc. as possible, not because the resultant practices are necessarily more appropriate than any others, but because they bring with them an enhanced position in the academic community. Linguists have had to pay attention to methodology, formulate all observations as rules, eschew (at least in theory) value judgement. The scientificness of linguistics is enshrined in three principles, which need to be introduced at the very beginning of our discussion.

1 Descriptive v. prescriptive: eliminating subjectivity

Linguistics is often described as 'the construction of *grammars*' but this is not the same sense of *grammar* as the one I mentioned earlier (rules for correct usage). Whilst most of us recall grammatical rules from English lessons at school – 'don't split infinitives' and 'never end a sentence with a preposition' for instance – these are exactly the sort of rules a linguist's grammar does not include. They are *prescriptive* rules telling people what they should say when they would naturally tend to say something else. The linguist is interested in *descriptive* rules, formulae which capture the regularities of what people really do say – or more accurately, because of a sophisticated theoretical sleight of hand which we will shortly come to, what they unconsciously *know* about their language. In other words, linguistic rules are laws of nature rather than rules of the game, to be discovered rather than invented. This is, of course, very nice for linguists who want to think of themselves as scientists.

At the bottom of the belief in description rather than prescription is the scientific requirement of objective investigation. Correctness in grammar is a social norm, arbitrary and based on value-judgement: therefore it cannot be the province of the objective scientist. To be objective, the linguist must include in her grammar not what ought to be said (e.g. *it is I*) but what *is* said (e.g. *it's me*), excluding only what cannot be said in the language under consideration (e.g. *it I is*). Many people have pointed out how erratically the distinction has been applied in practice, but it remains a basic principle. Comfortable in their reiterated assertion that prescription is a cardinal sin, most analysts do not bother with their own transgressions, still less ponder how far transgression may be unavoidable.

2 Synchronic v. diachronic: eliminating history

Before Saussure, the dominant approach to language study was comparative philology, which deals with relations between languages and traces their descent. Saussure thought that this historical approach stopped linguistics making a systematic analysis of language, since it dealt only with change through time, in his opinion an unsystematic phenomenon. Rather than watching the organism's development, he wanted to interrupt its life history and place it under the microscope in order to examine its internal structure. Therefore he proposed to cut through the time dimension at a particular point and study everything about the language as it existed in that frozen moment. He called this 'synchronic' linguistics, opposing it to 'diachronic' (historical) study.

Saussure obviously idealised the facts of language when he imagined cutting through a single moment in time, since languages are in a constant state of change. Moreover, in any speech community there exist forms from every point along the time dimension, because speakers vary in age. However, the idea that language could be studied ahistorically was an important one, and synchronic linguistics nowadays is not only distinguished from diachronic linguistics, it usually takes precedence over it.

3 Knowledge v. use: ordering chaos

The third important principle of linguistic science is the dichotomy between what the language user knows, the system, and the use she makes of that system as demonstrated by her actual linguistic behaviour. The data of speech are very complicated, heterogeneous to the point of chaos: so linguists propose that they must rest on something much more elegant and unified, a set of rules or relations which cannot be observed directly, but which may be inferred by the skilful scientist.

Saussure's version of this dichotomy is the *langue/parole* distinction. *Langue* is the abstract system of relations which make individual behaviour possible. It is a 'social contract' rather than the property of any one speaker, and it is the linguist's primary object of interest. The individual behaviour regulated by *langue*, particular instances of speech, is called *parole*. Chomsky too makes a knowledge/use distinction: in his case it is between *competence*, the set of rules known by native speakers of a language, and *performance*, the actual and imperfect language these speakers produce on the basis of the rules.

Both Chomsky and Saussure consider it more revealing to study *langue*, and to do so is now 'scientific' practice within linguistics.

Saussure's was the first theory to use fully the scientific principles of descriptiveness, synchronicity and knowledge orientation, and they have remained influential ever since. This is not to say, however, that Saussurean theory has dominated linguistics. The preoccupations of a science change according to the needs of the moment and the idea of science currently popular among intellectuals, and linguistics is no exception.

Three approaches to language study have arisen in linguistics which are relevant to our concerns, since all of them, and the contradictions between them, have implications for feminist theory. They are the structural approach, as exemplified by Saussure and later by the semiologists; the psychological approach, in which language is above all a property of the mind; and the sociocultural approach, which views language primarily as a product and a shaper of human culture.

THE STRUCTURAL APPROACH

Saussure

Many people regard Saussure as a 'thinker' rather than a linguist:

he is famous for having invented structuralism and founded the discipline of semiology. However, the major elements of his thought were developed expressly to deal with language, or more precisely, with his own abstraction, *langue*.

The defining characteristic of a structural approach is its insistence that language must be studied as a self-contained system, rather than, say, a historical phenomenon, a philosophical problem, a social or pedagogical tool. As Saussure put it, 'Language must...be studied in itself; heretofore language has almost always been studied in connection with something else, from other viewpoints.'[2] But if language is not just a tool of the mind, society, education or philosophy, what is left for it to be? Saussure's solution, from which all his theoretical insights sprang, was to view language as a sign system. He placed linguistics at the centre of a new science, the science of signs. 'A science that studied the life of signs within society is conceivable; it would be part of social psychology.... I shall call it semiology. Semiology would show what constitutes signs, what laws govern them.'[3] In other words, Saussure believed that within the field of social psychology lies a sub-field worthy of separate consideration: the tendency of human societies to construct symbolic systems such as languages. And indeed, this 'science' does now exist, having been brought to fruition by the neo-Saussurians, the semiologists of our own time.

What is a sign?

A sign is difficult to define adequately. It is what is produced by linking two theoretical entities, the signifier and the signified. In the case of language, Saussure exemplified the sign at the level of the word: so that the sign CAT, for instance, consists of a signifier which is the sound image /k a t/ and a signified which is the concept cat, a four-legged feline animal. In other words, we may say rather crudely that a signified is an idea, and the signifier what formally expresses it.

One important point about signs is that they separate language from things, from reality. A signified is not a thing, but a concept, and the sign is arbitrary in two ways. Firstly, signifiers are arbitrary. For there is nothing in nature which obliges a cat to be called a cat: it could just as easily have been called a BLERG, so long as the appropriate signified had been attached to that sequence of sounds. Equally, however, the signified is arbitrary; for prelinguistic reality (which exists for infants and those who cannot learn to speak, presumably) is an undifferentiated chaos out of which nothing naturally compels us to pick a class of CATS. By means of signs we make sense of a world that does not necessarily fall into neat conceptual classes; and in this process there is, according to Saussure, a great deal that is arbitrary.

Relations between signs

If signs are arbitrary, their substance does not matter much. What matters is that they should be distinguished from each other. It is the difference between signs that defines them.

This point may be grasped by thinking of military ranks such as private, corporal, sergeant, sergeant-major, etc. What do these mean without each other? If someone asks you what a private is, you are bound to reply that it is the lowest rank in the army, which means you are defining it in relation to other assumed ranks. Similarly, the signifiers of rank, stripes on a uniform, would be meaningless if they were not to be compared with each other.

Saussure talked about two sorts of relationship signs can have with each other. Either they can combine with each other (syntagmatic relations) like the sounds /k a t/ in CAT, or they can replace each other (associative or paradigmatic relations), as p, r, f, v, b, etc. could replace k in CAT.

American structuralism

An approach similar to Saussure's dominated American linguistics until the late 1950s. The American structuralist linguists were concerned with the actual description of native American languages on the verge of extinction, and their emphasis was on practical techniques for linguistic analysis.

The method they evolved was to describe a corpus, a sample of speech from a native speaker. Their grammars were inventories of the elements of a language (its sounds, words and grammatical forms) together with rules for the distribution of each element (i.e. where it could occur). Although not truly Saussurean, these linguists were structuralists in their approach and their analytic method.

SEMIOLOGY

Unlike American structuralism, semiology (a blanket term, as will become clear, for a number of rather different enterprises) *is* Saussurean: it is the 'science of signs' he suggested, and can only be defined as a single movement on the basis of its debt to the *Cours*. However, it is not thought of as part of the linguistic tradition, either by linguists or by its own practitioners, and to discuss the reasons why it is so different is to acknowledge a problem in the context of this book.

Theoretical linguistics as it exists now belongs to the predominantly Anglo-American scientific and social-scientific tradition. This tradition is bourgeois, empiricist and positivistic. In other words, for all that it has modified its objectives and methods since Saussure, linguistic theory remains locked within the view of 'science' that I have already outlined.

Semiology, on the other hand, exists within another tradition, not Anglo-American and scientific but French and literary. It is anti-bourgeois, anti-empiricist and sceptical about the mythology of science. Its own mythology is marxist and Freudian. In its aims, its methods and its general tone, it is unlike linguistics.

A somewhat similar gulf exists between feminism in France and in Britain or America. (This is an oversimplification, since dissenting voices are often heard, particularly among British intellectuals affected by the French tradition, but it is useful up to a point.) Marxism has affected both kinds of feminism, but whereas the English regard Freud as reactionary, the French are profoundly influenced in their feminism by psychoanalytic theory. They dislike our bourgeois empiricism, while we find their ideas over-theoretical and frequently biologistic (i.e. they attach more importance to the differences between women and men, often implying that these are the consequence of biology).

All this means that it is difficult, and perhaps illegitimate, to examine theories developed in the Anglo-American feminist and linguistic tradition alongside those developed in the French semiological context. These theories do not attempt to do the same things, either in terms of language or in terms of feminism: why should they be discussed in the same terms? How can I evaluate them when I belong irredeemably to the bourgeois empiricist camp?

In fact, it is far beyond the scope of this book to deal with semiology fully, and in particular I am neither concerned nor qualified to discuss the psychoanalytic basis of Lacanian theory. What interests me is the view of *language* semiologists hold, and specifically their analysis of the relation between language and women's oppression.

It is especially interesting that many Anglo-American writers who are *not* semiologists hold very similar views to the ones I am talking about. Some of them have been influenced by semiology, but others have derived the same ideas from quite different sources. This suggests two things: first, that something about women's experience of language makes certain ideas appealing, and secondly, that linguists and semiologists have something in common in the way they conceive of languages.

It follows that what I want to bring out when I discuss semiological theories is their similarities to linguistic theory, rather than the ways in which the two traditions differ. My discussion will be partial in both senses of the word; it will be directed to the three problems of sex-difference, sexism and alienation, asking whether semiology is useful to feminist theory rather than considering it entirely on its own terms.

SEMIOLOGY AND STRUCTURALISM

Although the terms *semiology* and *structuralism* are sometimes used as if they were interchangeable, in this book they are not.

Semiology is the field of study which Saussure envisaged and defined in the *Cours* as a science of signs − in other words, the investigation of symbolic systems such as languages. Thinkers like Lévi-Strauss, Barthes and Lacan (respectively an anthropologist, a literary critic and a psychoanalyst) are semiologists because they regard their objects of study (kinship, myth, the literary text, the unconscious) as sign-systems, organised as Saussure maintained languages are organised.

Structuralism, on the other hand, is a method for analysing phenomena, particularly sign-systems. It depends on the idea that differences and relationships are important, and although semiologists employ this method, it has also been employed without any concern for the theoretical framework of semiology.

In brief, then, semiology is a discipline and structuralism a method. When I mean the contemporary movement associated with the theories of Lacan, Derrida, Kristeva *et al.* I shall say *semiology*.

CULTURE AS SIGN-SYSTEM

It has already been explained how Saussure defined the system of signs; the system he was interested in was, of course, language. But clearly, it is not only language that consists of signs. The contemporary semiologists take Saussure's linguistic insights and apply them to other phenomena, treating diverse cultural objects and practices as sign-systems and studying them in the same way that Saussure studied language.

A short example of what this means in practice is provided by Roland Barthes' analysis of a magazine cover.[4] The photograph on this cover (in Saussurean terms the signifier) showed a black soldier saluting the French flag (its immediate meaning or signified). In Barthes' analysis, however, this sign (pairing of image and concept) was itself the signifier of a higher-order sign, the myth, whose signified was the idea of French imperialism as acceptable.

This kind of cultural analysis improves somewhat on the usual notions of stereotyping and representation by giving an account of why some images have a particular significance. Once an image becomes a sign, with its place in the network of relationships which is the system of signs, the union of signifier and signified which it embodies (out of many other possibilities) comes to be seen as natural and indissoluble.

The possible applications of this in feminist thinking are clear. It might be a possible explanation, for instance, of why one cannot normally use the signifier image of a naked woman without invoking in those who see it ideas of sexual availability and degradation. A naked woman does not signal those things inherently; in principle the image could mean many other things. Yet because it has become a sign, with the image as signifier and availability/degradation as signified, one particular meaning, a misogynist one, has more power than the alternatives, and its unpleasant connotations cannot simply be discarded.

We must be careful, however, not to argue that this kind of meaning is acquired in an arbitrary way. Certainly it is conventional, but it is mediated by the political structures of a misogynist society. In Barthes' example too, the sign can only be mythologised if we pay attention to a particular bit of it, the race of the soldier: and it is no accident that we do this, but a reflection of our culture's racism. In other words, signs are historically specific and signification does not occur in a vaccum.

Although some semiologists acknowledge this point, others are equivocal. This is because they have adopted a deterministic position, arguing that language creates all meanings within a society rather than reflecting, or interacting with, anything else. The kind of semiology feminists have been most influenced by, Lacanian psychoanalysis, is very deterministic; yet surely the question of *how* some images acquire political significance, and the nature of that significance, also deserves attention.

SEMIOLOGY AND PSYCHOANALYSIS

French feminism is strongly marked by the influence of psycho-analysis. In particular, many writers have developed their ideas in response to the psychoanalyst Jacques Lacan. The important thing about this is that Lacan's is a *linguistic* theory of the unconscious and of the subject's development: hence the critiques and reformulations which feminists have produced also centre on language, and have interesting things to say about language.

LACAN

In this introductory section my main objective is to explain *how* Lacan's psychoanalysic theory is 'linguistic,' and I shall not deal with its substance in detail.

Lacan is a semiologist because he regards the psychoanalyst's object of study, the unconscious, as a sign-system. He is deeply indebted to Saussure for many of his central concepts. Most important of all, Lacan's theory of the unconscious gives pride of place to language, thus producing a radical re-reading of Freud.

Lacan observes the stress which Freud put on language and linguistic evidence in his accounts of dreams and jokes. In case-histories too language is inevitably of the utmost importance, for the analyst has nothing else to go on when probing the analysand's unconscious. You cannot observe the unconscious: it is always mediated by language.

Following Saussure, Lacan believes that without language, everything must remain not only unobservable but undifferent-iated, without structure: and since (as Freud demonstrates) the unconscious is highly structured, it cannot exist before language does. Lacan reasons that the unconscious must in fact be constructed through language, as language develops in the child. This process governs and differentiates what is, before language, a mass of instinctual drives, an 'hommelette' (little man (*sic*)/omelette) spreading in all directions. For Lacan, then, it is learning language that makes us what we are; and since our sexuality and gender identity is an important component of what we are, his theory has important implications for feminists trying to understand how femininity is constructed in patriarchal societies.

THE PSYCHOLOGICAL APPROACH

Saussure believed that semiology was part of social psychology, and indeed no linguist has ever denied that language was somehow 'in the mind'. American structuralism, however, subscribed to the behaviouristic kind of psychology in which no attempt is made to study internal mental processes; and therefore the 'mental' aspects of language were given little emphasis in the major texts produced by American structuralist linguists.

The behaviourist position on language was attacked by Chomsky in his review of B.F. Skinner's *Verbal Behavior*.[5] Chomsky argued that the structures of language are too complicated for it to be learned by a stimulus-response mechanism motivated by positive reinforcement.

Chomsky also attacked the methods of American structuralism, because he believed linguistics should be not a set of procedures for analysing and classifying different languages, but a branch of cognitive psychology interested in the general properties of human language. These, in Chomsky's opinion, would be found nowhere but in the structure of the human mind itself. He objected that the traditional corpus was not only a violation of linguistic principle (being *parole* rather than *langue*) but an irrationality. For how could the description of a corpus provide an exhaustive account of the language? In any language, the number of sentences we can produce or understand is in principle infinite.

But how could anyone describe an infinite number of sentences? Chomsky answered this question with one of his own: how can anyone accomplish the child's task of *learning* an infinite number of sentences? Yet all normal children master a language.

Chomsky's belief that this impressive achievement could not be a matter of mere stimulus and response led him to three conclusions. First, he concluded that children do not learn sentences, but rules for producing sentences. These would be finite in number, though the sentences themselves are infinite. Secondly, he concluded that the rules must be innate in the child's mind: the structures of language are too complicated for children to pick up without some predisposition towards them. Thirdly, if language is somehow innate in humans, all languages must at some level be very like each other. Children learn to speak whatever they hear around them; whatever structures are innate, therefore, must apply to any human language.

There are several reasons to believe that linguistic abilities depend at least to some extent on an innate predisposition. Psychologically oriented linguists point to the features which differentiate human and animal languages, both structural (e.g. human languages are hierarchical) and communicational (it is possible to invent new messages, to lie, to talk about events removed in time and place, only in human languages).

It is also pointed out that human children show signs of being 'programmed' to learn language at a particular stage of development and in a particular way. 'Feral' children, who grow up away from society and are therefore not exposed to language at the critical period, find it very difficult to learn to speak subsequently regardless of their general intelligence.

The psychological approach in linguistics dictates that the

linguist should look not just for any set of rules which accurately describe a language, but for the set the child has in her brain. She must also pay attention to isolating linguistic universals, the features which, if Chomsky is right, all languages must share.

THE SOCIOCULTURAL APPROACH

The sociocultural approach to language views speaking as a mediator of social relations, a way of expressing social role, a reflection of, and an influence on, culture.

ANTHROPOLOGICAL LINGUISTICS

The American structuralists always had a particularly close connection with anthropology, because they necessarily combined the analysis of unfamiliar languages with the observation of unfamiliar cultures. In addition, many anthropologists have always been sensitive to the importance of language in regulating society: they have used linguistic data to pinpoint aspects of social organisation, and as a guide to what the people being studied regard as important. So a large cross-cultural literature has long been available on the social aspects of language.

One question which arose within the anthropological tradition has proved controversial: the problem of relativity and linguistic determinism. (Relativity expresses the idea that 'objective reality' is in fact perceived differently by different cultures or in different circumstances: determinism means that one particular agency is responsible for the variation.)

Some anthropological linguists believed that the extreme variations they observed in different peoples' perceptions of reality were directly attributable to language. For instance, a tenseless language like Hopi would make it impossible for its speakers to conceptualise time as speakers of English, a tense language, conceptualise it.

This theory is often called the *Sapir–Whorf hypothesis* after the two linguists most associated with it, Edward Sapir and Benjamin Lee Whorf. It is both relativistic (asserts that reality is perceived differently) and deterministic (asserts that language is responsible), and several recent feminist theorists acknowledge it has influenced them (e.g. Spender,[6] and Kramarae[6]) Determinist theories of language will be discussed in detail in Chapter 6.

SOCIOLINGUISTICS

The other major sociocultural trend in linguistics is sociolinguistics which emerged as a discipline in its own right during the 1960s. In its genesis several factors were at work, many of them very typical of the period.

First, there was a desire to study variation within languages in an up-to-date way. Dialectology, a historical and mainly rural subject, was not appropriate to study variation in the urbanised and geographically mobile society most linguists lived in, and a new sociological discipline was needed to analyse class and ethnic differences.

Secondly, many academics felt an impulse toward a more socially relevant linguistics, concerned with the problems of disadvantaged groups. (Needless to say, they usually ignored the largest such group – women.) A common motif in sociolinguistics is the description and defence of non-standard speech, and explicit opposition to educational theories blaming it for black and working class underachievement.

Thirdly, many sociolinguists believed that a different approach might make good worrying defects in the orthodox model of the time (i.e. Chomskyan transformational grammar). They wanted to show that a theory which excluded history and *parole* was artificial and unsatisfactory.

The technique of sociolinguistics is usually to correlate linguistic features in people's speech (different pronunciations and grammatical forms, for instance) with social indices like race, sex, age and class or with situational characteristics (how formal the situation is, what kind of speech event is taking place, etc.) In this, sociolinguistics might appear to be the linguistics of use and community rather than knowledge and the individual: yet paradoxically it claims to demonstrate, by showing that variations are structured and systematic rather than occurring at random, that these social aspects of language are as much part of our competence as the ability to construct grammatical sentences. A person who does not know how to vary her speech in different situations, or who cannot tell an old from a young speaker, is not a competent user of her language.

As well as subverting the knowledge/use distinction, sociolinguistics challenges the separation of synchronic and diachronic study. Many sociolinguists believe that they are interrelated, because it is the social significance of variation in the present which determines how language will change in the future.

SUMMARY

I do not want to imply that the three approaches discussed here are mutually incompatible in the sense that, for instance, structuralists think language is not a social phenomenon and sociolinguists see no cognitive/psychological element to be explained in language. It is quite possible to see all three approaches as valid and even useful. However, there are important inconsistencies, whose implications for feminism matter a good deal. For instance, the psychological linguist is committed to universalism and mentalism (belief in innate ideas) while to the sociolinguist it is more significant that languages and cultures vary. Whorfian determinism, which holds that the mind is deeply affected by the language it learns in the course of its development, cannot be reconciled with the Chomskyan view that all languages ultimately share one structure, dictated by properties of the human mind.

There are also tensions between the structual and sociocultural approaches. Practitioners of the latter believe that classical structuralism demands too much idealisation, the assumption of a homogeneity which no investigator will ever find in the real world of differences and, the sociolinguist reminds us, inequalities.

Lacan is interesting in that his theories synthesise all the approaches: structural in method, they are concerned both with psychological development and with the acculturation of individual subjects. But this synthesis is not without its problems, and Lacan would not be comfortable either with Chomsky or with Whorf. Although he shares the psycholinguist's belief that he is uncovering universal properties of the human mind, he does not believe in innate ideas; although his position is deterministic he seems not to be a relativist (which begs the question of how very different languages like English and Hopi can generate identical unconscious structures in their users).

These inconsistencies are relevant for feminist language study because to date its greatest debts have been to sociolinguistics and semiology. Both, in their feminist versions, are very deterministic, a position which is problematic and should not be accepted without question. On the other hand, where sociolinguistics stresses variation and heterogeneity, semiology pulls in the opposite direction toward a rigid and idealised systematicity which is far from anything we can observe. These are points to bear in mind, and they will be taken up again in the context of particular problems.

CONCLUSION

I want to conclude this chapter by indicating the contributions which the above approaches can make/have made to feminist language study.

Feminism and semiology

The contribution of semiology to feminist language study is a double one. First, there is its literary criticism, which has had a number of things to say about women's use of language in imaginative literature, female creativity, etc. I cannot give this aspect of semiology the attention it deserves, partly because I am not a literary critic or stylistician but also because to deal with literary writing would detract from my emphasis in his book.

The second contribution, however, is of more general interest to the linguist: it is the theory of 'gendered subjectivity' derived from Lacanian psychoanalysis. This amounts to a claim that women are alienated in society because they have to learn a male language, and it will be discussed in Chapter 7.

Feminism and sociolinguistics

Because it deals with language use in social context, sociolinguistics is by far the most fruitful source of data and work on sex-differences. Whatever the shortcomings of prefeminist surveys (see Chapter 3), they did sample the speech of a large number of women. In recent years, a great deal of research on sex-difference has actually been done by feminists, who are attracted to sociolinguistics precisely because within it they can work on the questions which relate to women and language.

Another contribution which sociolinguistics can make to our understanding as feminists concerns the relation between language and disadvantage. The last decade has produced a considerable literature on speech, social evaluation and deprivation/underachievement. Almost all of it concerns either racial minorities or the working class (groups which, astonishingly; successive researchers have chosen to represent with all-male samples) but the findings are suggestive and could well be helpful to students of female oppression.

Feminism and anthropological linguistics

Anthropology's most significant contributions to feminist thinking about language have been theoretical, since it has given us both the Sapir–Whorf hypothesis and the 'dominant/muted' theory of Edwin and Shirley Ardener (both extensively used by feminists). It demonstrates a very helpful concern with the role of language in thought and culture. Anthropological studies allow us to see how far linguistic means are used to maintain the social order in other cultures, and this suggests interesting parallels with our own (for instance sexist language as verbal violence; restrictions on women speaking in public as a form of social control; judgements on speech style as reinforcements of sexist personality theories).

In addition, anthropology provides cross-cultural data on sex differences which is of interest both linguistically and as an insight into other societies' sexual politics.

Feminist linguistics?

Finally, it is difficult to separate the contribution these approaches can make to feminist theory from the things feminism can teach linguistics. In so far as linguists have dealt with the language of/about women, feminists must scrutinise their work and present a careful critique. I shall begin on this in the next chapter, which is about sex difference.

3   The Politics of Variation: Sex Differences in Language and Linguistics

> In a society where women are
> devalued it is not surprising
> that their language should be
> devalued. . . .

Dale Spender

Although this chapter is about sex differences in language, it is not intended to serve as a catalogue of research findings. Rather, it has two main concerns: the first, which it shares with Chapter 4, is the sexism of linguistic science, as expressed by a mass of assumptions and practices reflecting the status quo; while the second is the political significance of sex difference itself. Hence the chapter heading is deliberately ambiguous, referring not only to the politics of variation but also to the politics of studying it.

Feminists have frequently pointed out that the study of sex differences in any subject has a political dimension, and that many sex difference studies are simply elaborate justifications of female subordination (girls don't become engineers because they are inferior to boys on tests of spatial ability) or else overt anti-feminist propaganda (as in the recent rise of sociobiology, which sets out to prove that the domestication of women is a biological imperative, determined by our genes). Sex difference research inevitably comes out of sexist ideology, and its findings, unsurprisingly, are interpreted in ways that reinforce that ideology. There is usually a hidden presumption (if indeed the experimenters trouble to hide it) that men are the norm from which women deviate, that the male norm is superior to the female deviation, and that the difference is ultimately reducible to biology, that is, 'natural'.

Hence an honourable feminist tradition has arisen of directing our scholarly attention to the academic explanation of sex difference rather than to difference itself. The aim is to expose, and then to destroy, academic legitimations of women's oppression, which are a powerful force simply because so many people accept the factuality and objectivity of science.

In linguistics, however, this has not been such a major feminist concern. Sneering at long dead researchers like Jespersen and Sapir has become a commonplace, but a thorough feminist critique of modern sociolinguistics has been much slower to emerge. (There are some useful comments in this direction by Jenkins and Kramarae, a few of which will be developed here.)[1] In general, feminists within linguistics have been more interested in furthering the study of sex difference than in criticising it. It is interesting to ask why this should be the case. What have feminists to gain from studying sex differences in language?

A survey of the studies carried out by feminist linguists suggests there are two main motives (which are not mutually incompatible and may occasionally co-occur). The first is the quest for an 'authentic' female speech or writing, whether this is taken to reflect some deep-seated cognitive or unconscious difference, or the existence in specific societies of distinctive female subcultures. The political point of this approach is to isolate and validate a female mode of language use, and to relate such a variety (supposing it exists) to the general notion of female culture.

The second motive has more to do with identifying the sexual power dynamic in language use. Here, sex differences in language are related to the power of men and the powerlessness of women, and the political point being made is that even our speech behaviour reflects and perpetuates patriarchal norms.

Feminist sex difference researchers in linguistics have therefore addressed themselves to a number of questions. How great are the verbal differences between men and women? Are they great enough, for instance, to justify us in talking about separate languages or dialects ('genderlects') for the sexes? Are the differences innate, reflecting anatomical or cognitive factors, or are they learned? At what stage of development do they arise? Finally, what can we learn from the substance of the differences? Are they best understood as expressing a feminine identity, as functions of the particular social/occupational roles taken by women in particular societies, or simply as the indices of oppression and powerlessness? What is their over-all significance?

These are the very same questions that any account of linguistic variation would have to deal with, feminist or not. Although the feminist and the anti-feminist favour different explanatory strategies, they share a belief that in language use we have a key to the nature and relative status of the sexes.

In this chapter then, I propose to look at how sex differences in language reflect, or are said by researchers to reflect, the nature (or role) and status of women and men. As well as pointing out the obvious biases and blind spots in current models, I shall also be trying to demonstrate the problems raised by this idea that language use is a direct reflection of social identity. The explanation of linguistic behaviour and linguistic variation is trickier either than feminists suppose, or than linguists admit.

SEX DIFFERENCE STUDIES: A CRITIQUE

Linguistic accounts of sex difference are open to criticism on three fronts. First, we may be critical of the way the field has been set up, so that women's speech is viewed only as a collection of deviations from the (male) norm. Secondly, we may be highly suspicious of most studies' actual findings (if that is the right term for anecdotes, stereotypes and survey results distorted by methodological bias). Thirdly, we must take up the matter of interpretation and explanation in some detail. For once again, sex difference studies do not describe male and female attributes without comment. Undertaken by people who share the prejudices of their culture, they end up rationalising and perpetuating those prejudices.

DELIMITING THE FIELD: WHAT IS SEX DIFFERENCE?

It might seem at first glance that every question about language and sex is a question of sex difference, but for the linguist the concept is more limited. It goes back to the important distinction in linguistics between system and use, *langue* and *parole*: sociolinguistics, the subdiscipline that deals with sex difference and with linguistic variation in general, concerns itself not with generic *he*, terms of insult and other things that are 'in the language', but only with variations in people's linguistic behaviour.

Sex differences exist for the linguist, then, when a linguistic feature (for instance rising intonation or the word *darling*) is used significantly more by one sex than the other: or when people's linguistic norms and standards are different for women and for men (for instance, it is less acceptable for women to swear).

This statistical concept of difference defines all pre-feminist (and some feminist) research into women's talk. It might seem obvious that in order to study the speech of any group, one would observe and record its members and then produce a full description: but in the sociolinguistic paradigm the favoured method is in fact comparative, requiring the researcher to describe most varieties only in terms of how they differ from other varieties (in practice, from a white, male, standard middle-class norm). Thus from Jespersen in 1922 to Labov in 1972, women's speech was dealt with only in so far as it diverged from men's.

This norm-and-deviation research framework, as I shall shortly argue, is an important factor in producing both stereotyped findings about women, and stereotypical explanations. Yet the emergence and dominance of this framework is not surprising, since the sociolinguists with their hidden norms are the natural heirs of a long tradition in the study (and indeed the lay discussion) of linguistic variation – a tradition we might call the 'anecdotal' or 'folklinguistic' in which the speech of subordinate groups is represented first as different, and then as deviant, from the standard. This tradition goes back to Antiquity: where sex differences are concerned, it persists both inside and alongside modern sociolinguistics.

THE ANECDOTAL TRADITION: WOMEN AND FOLKLINGUISTICS

'Folklinguistics' is the name given to that collection of beliefs about language which are accepted as common sense within a society. These beliefs serve both to regulate linguistic behaviour, and to explain it to the ordinary language user; some of them are fairly accurate, some quite false. Within folklinguistics it is possible to isolate 'stereotypes', popular pictures of the speech of particular groups. Once again, these representations may be accurate in linguistic terms (for instance, the well-known observation that Birmingham accents are 'nasal') or they may be wrong (for instance, the idea that Cockney glottal stops are 'sloppy'). The value judgements implied in many stereotypes fit rather well with the relative power and social prestige of the groups concerned.

One way of muddying the waters in sex difference studies is not to make a distinction between false stereotype sex differences and ones for which there is good evidence. Many linguists apparently do not realise how far 'value-free' observations are in fact conditioned by a long history of misogynist folklinguistics. This ignorance is all the more unfortunate because stereotypes of women's talk are so inaccurate; and even the most ludicrous beliefs return to haunt 'empirical' sociolinguistics.

An amusing early example of the kind of stereotype we are discussing comes from Jonathan Swift's 1712 'Proposal for Correcting the English Tongue'. Swift asserts that some sounds are typical of men, others of women:

> ... if the Choice had been left to me, I would rather have trusted the Refinement of our Language ... to the Judgement of the Women, than of illiterate Court-Fops, half-witted Poets and University Boys. For it is plain, that in their Manner of corrupting Words, Women do naturally discard the Consonants, as we do the Vowels ... more than once, where some of both Sexes were in Company, I have persuaded two or three of each to take a Pen, and write down a Number of Letters joined together, just as it came into their Heads: and upon reading this Gibberish we have found that which the Men had writ, by the frequent encountering of rough Consonants to sound like High Dutch, and the other by the Women, like Italian, abounding in Vowels and Liquids. Now, although I would by no Means give Ladies the trouble of advising us in the Reformation of our Language, yet I cannot help thinking, that since they have been left out of all Meetings, except Parties at Play, or where worse Designs are carried on, our Conversation hath very much degenerated.[2]

Everyone can laugh at this, and no one now would take it seriously. But equally silly proposals are to be found in serious works of linguistic scholarship that date from our own century.

The paradigm example here, invariably slated by feminist commentators, is Otto Jespersen's extraordinary chapter on 'The Woman' in his 1922 book, *Language: Its Nature, Development and Origin*.[3] Although Jespersen is sometimes accused of misogyny, his chapter reveals him as a gallant rather than a male chauvinist; and it is remarkable not so much for its anti-feminism as for the obvious conviction of its author that no evidence is required to back up his assertions about the way women speak. Readers will simply recognise, Jespersen implies, that women really do speak more softly than men, use diminutives like *teeny-weeny*, construct their sentences 'loosely' and leave them unfinished, all the while jumping from topic to topic.

These characteristics predicated of women were evidently not chosen at random. Jespersen is caught between his fantasies (soft-spoken, retiring child-women) and his prejudices (loquacious but illogical bird-brains) to produce a sexist stereotype which is still recognisable sixty years on. Cartoon humour still revolves around women's verbal incontinence ('When two wives get together, who has the last word?' enquires Andy Capp) though recent findings indicate that men actually talk a great deal more than women when both sexes are present at the same time. Illogical women who can't keep to the point also surface in media representations of folk-wisdom ('You might as well try to knit fog as follow what's in a woman's mind' says a character in *Coronation Street*). As for *teeny-weeny* and its childish analogues, I have heard them placed firmly in the female lexicon as recently as July 1982.[4]

Stereotypes, however false, tend to persist for as long as they reinforce important social inequalities. So long as women are subordinate to men, their language has got to be characterised as indicating natural subservience, unintelligence and immaturity. While men dominate women in mixed groups by limiting their opportunity to talk, our folklinguistic beliefs must include the untruth that women talk incessantly.

Unfortunately, not all inaccurate stereotypes have been rejected even by feminists. The first book to alert linguists to the political implications of sex differences, Robin Lakoff's *Language and Woman's Place*, itself creates a new stereotype.[5] According to Lakoff, women use more tag-questions ('approval-seeking' constructions of the 'that'll be all right, won't it?' type) and more rising intonation, which according to Lakoff indicates uncertainty. They use intensifiers like *really* and *very* more than men do, and approximators such as *a bit, not exactly*. The picture that emerges from *Language and Woman's Place* is of a subservient way of talking where nothing is asserted outright, and everything is qualified.

Lakoff is a feminist, and she explains the differences she discusses in political terms. Women use approval-seeking constructions because they need to seek approval, and fear that men would find a bare statement threatening or offensive. Nevertheless, Lakoff's picture is a stereotype for which she presents no real evidence, and other women who have tested her hypothesis against a quantity of speech data have found it wanting on several counts.

Dubois and Crouch, for instance, tested the hypothesis that women use more tag-questions than men. In their sample, on the contrary it was men who used more than women.[6] (Tag-questions will be discussed below, for they provide a good example of what needs to be avoided in sex difference research.)

Why do stereotypes like this persist in modern 'scientific' linguistics? Partly it has to do with the methods used. Lakoff was trained in the Chomskyan tradition, which, as I pointed out in Chapter 1, rejected the idea of collecting a sample corpus, advising instead that the analyst examine her own intuitions about language. Obviously this is not satisfactory when your analysis involves large-scale generalisations about the linguistic behaviour of groups; and there is a problem about asking others for their intuitions. It has been found that people consistently misreport their own behaviour when they are asked to describe it. They report usages that owe more to the stereotype than to the truth.

Feminists too have strong folklinguistic beliefs about women's speech. This is not itself surprising: what is striking, however, is the extent to which feminist beliefs resemble those put forward by linguists whose political views are the opposite of feminist. It sometimes seems as if feminists took their stereotype straight from the pages of Jespersen, and this raises the interesting question of the origin and importance of folklinguistic beliefs generally.

INVESTIGATING FEMINIST FOLKLINGUISTICS

In the feminist workshops, seminars and group discussions on language that I have attended, several folklinguistic assertions have been made over and over again. From them I have put together a profile of women's speech with the following six features:

1. Disfluency (because women find it hard to communicate in a male language).
2. Unfinished sentences.
3. Speech not ordered according to the norms of logic.
4. Statements couched as questions (approval-seeking).
5. Speaking less than men in mixed groups.
6. Using co-operative strategies in conversation, whereas men use competitive strategies.

This is how feminists believe women typically speak, and there is a tendency to make these attributes the basis of an authentic 'women's style' which would be positively valued. As with many other things, so with language: women are saying 'we do it differently, and our way is just as good as yours'.

Revaluing the things that are distinctively female may well be a significant and necessary political act. However, there is little point in revaluing a speech style that exists only in the folklinguistic imagination. Therefore it seems rather important to investigate whether women do in fact leave their sentences unfinished, couch their statements as questions, use co-operative strategies and so on: and to look a little more closely at what such characteristics may or may not mean.

In the discussion that follows, I have used real data from surreptitiously recorded conversation to illustrate the difficulties of investigation and interpretation. Some of the data comes from a discussion on sex education between two male friends;[7] some of it comes from a discussion on nuclear disarmament between two female friends; and the remainder comes from a tape on which I recorded the opinions of six women on male and female speech styles.

It is clear from the six points of the folklinguistic profile (above) that feminists are more interested in large-scale abstractions (how women communicate, express themselves) than in the sociolinguist's orderly matrix of micro-variables (e.g. the incidence of particular vowel qualities or grammatical constructions). They make impressionistic comments like the following:

Women try and make it interesting, you know, make you

want to listen, men just bash on regardless, they expect you to listen.

Men are so competitive when they talk, it's not like what I would call a conversation, it's like – well, a competition.

There were some women there who were really well informed politically, one woman really talked a lot – God, isn't it awful, if it's a woman you say to your friends, didn't so-and-so talk a lot! And men, well it happens all the time, some man just goes on and on and you never say a thing . . .

'I used to really worry about saying things in a logical order, because the men would say I wasn't putting it in a logical order . . .'

But this raises two enormous problems for linguistic researchers. First, what should we look for by way of evidence for impressionistic labels like 'logical order', 'competitiveness' and 'making it interesting'? Secondly, if we find the more straightforwardly identifiable elements of the profile in women's speech (unfinished sentences for instance), how are we to check the accompanying feminist explanations? These problems can be illustrated by taking each of the six elements in turn.

Disfluency, meaning pauses, hesitations, false starts, repetitions and so on, is relatively easy to quantify in a piece of linguistic data. However linguists do not agree on what it actually means. Some of them see pausing as a strategy speakers use to plan what they are going to say next, and argue that those who do not pause often are thoughtless or unintelligent (this argument has been used about working-class speakers by Bernstein, and about women by Jespersen). Others believe that disfluencies are a sort of mistake that people have special ways of repairing; while yet others believe that discontinuity in speech is a stylistic device that people use for effect to convey particular messages. So if there is a sex difference in fluency, there is still a problem of interpretation.

Unfinished sentences, similarly, present difficulties before we even get to sex differences. For the complete sentence is not in fact the most usual unit of conversation, and we are misled by the conventions of writing into asserting the supremacy of something which is not the norm. Typical utterances in a conversation use pausing and intonation to make their meaning clear, rather than 'perfect' sentential syntax:

> and also – also the only way they could probably swing an election behind them, that would be the issue . . .

> well what do you think about sex education do you think that er it er I mean there's been a great hooha about it recently hasn't there . . .

These utterances are not at all confusing, but they are also not much like the sentences one learns to write at school. Nor is it clear what producing a high proportion of utterances that 'tailed off' would mean in terms either of cognition or of social confidence.

Logic in speech is a very inexact notion, and could in addition refer either to the content of what is said, or to the sequencing of what is said ('logical ORDER').I suspect that linguists like Jespersen have the first possibility in mind when they accuse women of illogic, while feminists, in rejecting male speech structures, are thinking more of the second. But in any case, what do we mean by logic?

Consider two extracts from the data.

(1) B: I must say I tend to be . . . I mean I . . . you know I do talk quite openly to my pupils which is a little daring of me because the situation in Cyprus is different from here . . . I mean people are a bit narrow in that respect you know they don't like people to talk about it too openly – but I do because I think it's important but the trouble is that – erm – that's not really systematic in the sense that I do it but how many people – how many other people do it you see.

    A: Yes it's er it's an enormous problem actually because as soon as you start to make a special thing about it then immediately I think you're creating the wrong atmosphere, especially for sex.

(2) C: I'd sell my soul to get nuclear weapons out of Britain.

    D: Well I don't think you're ever going to get it except by civil disobedience because it's part of what a government's all about, they have to defend the country. I don't think getting the Labour Party to resolve for unilateral disarmament changes anything ... they just won't put it into practice they can't ... you look at the record of governments there's no way they can stop defending us.

C: I think that there's some hope now with the Labour Party because they've um compromised themselves politically so far that they wouldn't –

The second extract might be judged in many ways more overtly logical than the first. Its structure could be shown like this:

- nuclear weapons should be got rid of (opinion);
- the only way to do it is through civil disobedience (suggestion);
- because governments have to defend their country, so party political promises of disarmament change nothing (justification of suggestion);
- look at the record of governments (evidence for justification);
- nevertheless there is hope through getting the Labour Party to commit itself (disagreement)
- because it would be politically disadvantageous to break a promise (justification).

The argument progresses without a break and has all the hallmarks of logic (e.g. careful justification, the bringing in of evidence, the overt statement of opinion and disagreement).
  The first extract is less simple.

- I talk to my pupils openly about sex (statement);
- this is daring (evaluation);
- because in Cyprus they aren't keen for people to be that open (justification).
- But I think it's important (justification of the first point);
- the trouble is I don't do it systematically (evaluation of the first point);
- but no one else does it at all (justification putting evaluation in perspective);
- sex education is an enormous problem (opinion);
- because making a thing of it creates the wrong atmosphere for discussing sex (justification of opinion).

  Speaker B's logic does not proceed in an unbroken chain but returns to deal with the same point (the first point) in a number of different ways. Although A starts with *yes*, indicating that he will take up B's points, in fact he is off on another tack altogether, and what he says is connected to what has gone before only loosely, by the general subject of sex education.

So although there is logic in this extract (and there's no reason why speakers should not change their tack, since this gives conversation its vitality), it is not so clearly logical as the other extract.

As these conversational samples show, logic in conversation does not have to consist in making each utterance follow rigidly from the last. Complex interconnections, doubling back on yourself and so on, can be easy to understand in context.

The philosopher H.P. Grice once devised a framework for talking about logic in conversation.[8] He suggested that speakers and hearers follow a number of conventions known collectively as the 'co-operative principle', namely: give as much information as is required, and no more; give true information or information for which you have evidence; be relevant; don't be vague, ambiguous or prolix. If a speaker breaks one of these maxims in an obvious way, either her utterance will be examined more closely by the hearer, or else the hearer will derive some hidden inference. In other words, if people deviate from the maxims, their hearers still try to make the contribution sensible and logical. They assume the speaker had a good reason for her deviant behaviour, and they set out to discover what it was. So long as hearers believe speakers are being relevant, truthful, informative and so on, conversation will flow in a logical way. If hearers suspect speakers are not being relevant, truthful and informative, perplexity will ensue. Hence in this sample, the sequence

how many other people do it you see
Yes it's an enormous problem

is perfectly logical to the participants, though out of context the connection may not be clear. On the other hand, in the conversation from which extract 2 is taken we have this:

C: Was she at Styal
D: She came out yesterday
C: She was at Styal

D: no she was in first Drake Hall.

C does not take 'she came out yesterday, as a logical reply to 'was she at Styal' because it is not informative enough. She therefore checks up by repeating her question as an assertion, which D then denies. To the observer it might seem logical to infer from 'she came out yesterday' that the answer *Yes* is presupposed: but for some reason, C does not make this 'logical' inference, and she turns out to be right.

What needs to be pointed out here is the uselessness of applying inflexible notions of logic to so flexible an instrument as conversation. All conversations viewed in context (i.e. taking into account the shared knowledge of the participants and the situation in which they are talking) exhibit strong logical connections, and on the other hand, all speakers and hearers make use of essentially extra-logical devices, particularly the affective cues carried in tone of voice.

It is hard to see that looking for systematic differences in people's construction of spoken texts would be a feasible or useful insight into sex difference. So what is the source of the belief, held in common by chauvinists and feminists, that women's speech is less logical than men's? At this point we may consider two suggestions, to which later chapters will return. The first is that in some modes of discourse – public speaking for example – a very explicit logical sequencing might be more appropriate than it is in ordinary casual conversation. These are precisely the speech modes used less by women than by men, because of restrictions on women's participation in formal speech events.

The second is more interesting. Since the logic of ordinary conversation is determined by the participants and may be implicit in the knowledge they share rather than being objectively inspectable from the outside, groups with little shared knowledge will find it hard to follow each other's conversation. Men and women, with their differing roles and experiences, do not have perfect shared knowledge, and the interactions of one sex are mysterious to the other. As usual, however, the more powerful group (men) have the right to make authoritative value-judgements, and thus to label women's talk 'illogical', backed up by the old stereotype of inherent female irrationality in every sphere.

Cheris Kramarae discusses the possibility that women have to become attuned to the dynamics of male conversation, whereas men do not have the same obligation *vis-à-vis* women.[9] In that case the bafflement caused by a lack of shared knowledge would be peculiar to the male sex.

It is interesting to note that subordinate groups are very often accused of speaking in an 'illogical' way. Thus educational psychologists in the 1960s contended that the speech of Black American ghetto children was 'a basically non-logical form of expressive behavior'. Linguistic analysis revealed that the speech in question had different structural rules, which simply had not been understood by the white educators. Yet because it is the prerogative of the powerful to evaluate everyone else, the 'illogical' label could be appended and used to disparage Black American speakers.

The search for logic in language is, in itself, rather uninteresting. In some ways language is very much a logical system, so that a totally illogical language could not be an efficient communication medium; while on the other hand it is hard to imagine a natural language logical in the style of the propositional calculus. But the uses to which the lay concept of logic in language has been put are political, and for that reason feminists must be concerned to debunk it.

Perhaps the most widely held feminist idea about women's speech is that whereas men compete in conversation, women use co-operative strategies. This is by no means easy to investigate. However, certain investigators have tried to devise frameworks in which to look at how people establish hierarchies and make decisions through talk.

For instance, R.F. Bales designed such a framework for the analysis of people's interaction in conferences.[10] Bales trained observers to code everything that was said with labels such as the following: requesting opinion, requesting information, putting forward opinion, putting forward information, expressing agreement, expressing solidarity, expressing disagreement, expressing antagonism. There are at least two major difficulties with any framework of this kind. The first is a coding difficulty. Situations might very well arise where the observer was unsure which of two categories to put some utterance into. Bales used a number of analysts and (presumably) looked for agreement amongst them, but this suggests he was investigating the metalinguistic abilities of his observers at least as much as he was investigating the linguistic behaviour of the conference participants.

Secondly, there is a problem with the sensitivity of the framework to situations. Suppose one hypothesised that co-operative conversationalists would produce a lot of requests for opinions (bringing others into the discussion) and express solidarity or agreement frequently. How could the investigator allow for the possibility that opinions may be requested antagonistically (for instance, by picking on someone who has no desire to speak) or that in many kinds of interaction it is normal for agreement or solidarity to be expressed as part of a more general strategy of criticism or contradiction?

In this particular sample, it appeared that the women speakers were notably less co-operative (in so far as that term can be defined; as I have just pointed out, a lot of qualifications and ad hoc judgements have to be made when we try to apply any general framework). While both sexes requested approximately equal amounts of information and opinion, expressed a good deal of agreement and no antagonism, women interrupted more, disagreed more, and back channelled less.

The reason for this unexpected finding seems fairly obvious. It happens that in the data specimen I chose, the men are discussing a subject on which they agree. The women, in contrast, do not agree with each other. A number of facts in the situation determine whether the participants will be 'co-operative' or 'competitive', notably, if banally, whether they agree, whether they like each other, what they are trying to accomplish in talk and so on. Conversation is a highly contextualised phenomenon, and to generalise about it on the basis of so gross a variable as speaker sex is unwise.

Why, then, does the stereotype of competitive men and co-operative women seem so ingrained in feminist folklinguistics (and indeed in linguistics, in so far as women's conversational strategies have been studied at all)? Are feminists deluding themselves about women's less aggressive nature? Are they picking up and revaluing the stereotype men have of women as 'good listeners'? Perhaps both these things play a part in the creation of this particular stereotype. But I think there is one other factor, and that is the extremely co-operative style which has been institutionalised in feminist gatherings. In such gatherings it is conveyed to participants that they should not interrupt nor raise their voices to silence others, that solidarity should be expressed frequently, that women must give way to each other rather than competing for the floor, and so on. Long silences are tolerated.

This style was worked out painstakingly to avoid advantaging relatively more 'articulate' (i.e. middle-class and educated) women. That it is a feminist and not a female norm is suggested by remarks my women informants have made to me about it:

'I had a lot of trouble not interrupting, I felt everyone was thinking I couldn't keep my mouth shut.'

'It struck me the minute we started, all the silence and letting people finish.'

Although there are obvious political justifications for the 'feminist style' I am talking about, it is interesting that many feminists justify its peculiarities differently. They tell you it is a style that 'suits women better' or gets away from 'male ways of speaking'. In other words, though the history and anecdote of early second-wave feminist suggests a difficult and painful process of working out a suitable style, under considerable pressure from women who had not been trained to speak in public, this process has already been obliterated and the style has become naturalised. Once again, the power of the folklinguistic in explaining and regulating usage is unmistakable.

Linguists too may have helped to further the idea, if not of women as co-operators then at least of men as competitors. It is very noticeable that studies of all-male interaction (for instance the classic Harlem studies of William Labov) tend to look at large-scale ritual performances within hierarchical groups, whereas studies of women focus on small groups in intimate conversations. This is surely simplistic. Even if fewer women than men participate in groups and gangs, is it really true that men do not have intimate conversations? Or are sociolinguists subconsciously influenced in their choice of data by their own folk and folklinguistic beliefs about the activities and social organisation typical of women and men?

The anecdotal tradition is not, of course, without interest. On the contrary, it is essential that a feminist account of language take into consideration people's beliefs about male and female speech, for the prejudice is often more powerful than the fact. However, as many linguists have pointed out, a study of sex differences cannot rely on anecdotes and stereotypes. It must substantiate claims about women's usage with empirical evidence (not forgetting that women of different ages, regional, class and ethnic backgrounds cannot be dealt with in one breath) and that evidence must be based not on what men say women say, or what women say they say, but on what they really do say.

The branch of linguistic enquiry which claims to approach sex difference in this empirical spirit is modern sociolinguistics. We must now ask whether sociolinguistic studies have improved on anecdotal accounts of women's speech.

WOMEN AND SOCIOLINGUISTICS

The major approach to social differences in speech is the large-scale sociolinguistic survey. A representative sample of the target population (determined by the sociological techniques of stratified or random sampling) is interviewed, and recordings are analysed. Linguistic features of various sorts are then correlated with social characteristics such as age, gender, ethnicity and class.

This kind of survey has been done in a number of urban areas, including New York City, Norwich, Tyneside and Belfast. The usual focus of interest is 'social stratification', the correlation of how often certain items of grammar or pronounciation are used with socioeconomic class. For instance, in New York there is a stratification pattern for the alternation of *that* and *dat*. The lower your socioeconomic class, the more likely you are to use the non-standard pronounciation *dat* rather than standard *that*. Stratification is also observable in situations of varying formality: the more formal the occasion, the more the standard will be used by members of every socioeconomic group.

It has been argued (e.g. by Pellowe *et al.*) that stratification mania does nothing but confirm stereotypes.[11] Investigators are so keen to draw the magic stratification graph, they fail to look beyond the handful of features that produce it. And these features are, of course, the obvious ones that everyone already knows. Pellowe believes that in concentrating on the blindingly obvious, linguists risk missing complex variation which is equally important.

Feminist linguists have also criticised the stratification approach:

> Both the theory and the methodology are based on the implicit assumption that the communicative experience of white middle class males is prototypical . . . the experience of women, other ethnic groups and classes are treated as deviations.[12]

Nowhere is the tendency to simplistic norm-and-deviation models clearer than in one theory that has emerged from sociolinguistic survey findings, social marker theory (Scherer and Giles).[13] In effect, this theory says that people's speech contains features that mark them out as belonging to particular social groups. Some of these features are so consciously attended to by hearers that they figure in popular stereotypes, while others have to be isolated by the linguist.

In principle this has a certain merit, since it acknowledges that there is variation beyond the stereotype and that the correlations language-users make between linguistic and social indices are very complex. Yet in practice social marker theory is afflicted with the same shortcomings we have seen in surveying: researchers do concentrate on the variations that have an overt significance for language users, and they do tend to define a marker as a feature distinguishing its user's speech from an implicit norm. The recognition that someone is a white middle-class male, for instance, is assumed to depend on the absence of markers.

There are three objections to the norm and deviation framework of sociolinguistics. First, researchers notoriously find what they set out to find, and if all they are looking for is gross and salient differences perceived by everyone, that is all they will find. Secondly, if there is an implicit norm, non-standard varieties will tend to be described as collections of deviations rather than as integrated systems. Thus the question of how far they are or are not integrated systems in their own right cannot even be addressed. Third, the researcher working in this framework will feel the need to explain why women or blacks deviate from men/whites, but not vice versa. In other words, it is thought that non-standard varieties have special qualities requiring explanation, whereas white male speech is entirely unremarkable.

It is the matter of explaining that I want to concentrate on. For not only is there intellectual confusion in deciding just what variations need an explanation, the explanations themselves are frequently very objectionable. As Jenkins and Kramarae observe, 'Gender, ethnicity and class are seen as "demographic variables" which can be controlled and accounted for, often by using ad hoc explanations based on cultural stereotypes.'[14]

THE SOCIOLINGUISTIC EXPLANATION OF SEX DIFFERENCE

Sex differences in language are particularly susceptible to being treated as deviations requiring explanation, for a number of reasons (all of which rest ultimately on the notion that however large the female population may be – and in our culture it is more than 50 per cent – it is men who are normal, not women).

Women, unlike blacks or workers, do not in most western cultures form a separate community. This marginalises them from the start, since although they are at least half the population, in patriarchal society they can easily sink out of sight. In particular, no large *public* community of women draws attention to their existence as a group. Connected to this is the fact that male and female varieties of language are not normally analysed as products of differing histories and cultures, since women's history and culture is thought to be subsumed in men's. This factor distinguishes the language of women from the language of minority ethnic groups and many English regional varieties, which have an acknowledged tradition and often a flourishing culture too.

But in any case, how far can we speak of 'women's languages' or 'genderlects' in the same way we can talk of 'Yorkshire dialect' or 'black English'? Before we turn to English, it is helpful to look at a case where linguists thought for many years they were dealing with separate male and female languages. It is from cases like this that we get the concepts still used now in the explanation of sex difference.

Carib

The community that raised this problem for linguistics is the Carib Indians. Here women and men were reported in 1665 to use different phonologies (sound systems) and lexicons (vocabulary). The missionaries who originally observed this phenomenon gave a historical justification. According to them, the island had been invaded by the neighbouring Arawak tribe, who exterminated the male Caribs and kept the women only for reproductive purposes. Both sexes retained the languages they had spoken originally, mothers passing Carib on to their daughters, while fathers taught Arawak to their sons.

Later linguists, however, preferred an explanation based on gender role rather than biological sex. Noting a gender-based division of labour, analysts argued that women and men had developed different lexicons because they did different things. Jespersen elaborated this with a description of 'primitive society': while men, out hunting, developed a language of sparse and economical remarks designed to co-ordinate activity, women indulged in idle chatter at home. Jespersen here sets a high standard for sexist non-explanation, but his emphasis on *role* has become standard in sociolinguistic explanation.

Social marker theory distinguishes between two types of sex marker, the sex-exclusive (where certain features are used only by one sex, as in the Carib case) and the sex-preferential (where features are common to both sexes, but are more likely to be used by one sex than the other). In the case of sex-preferential markers in particular, there may be a strong correlation with occupation rather than with being a man or a woman *per se*.

A simple example from our own culture is 'motherese', the language women use to young children, which has a distinctive lexicon and features like high pitch, loudness, slowness and exaggerated intonational contours. It is a sex-preferential variety, used much more by women than by men. But this is just because women, rather than men, take care of children. In so far as men have anything to do with childcare, they too can be observed to use motherese.

Sex-exclusive markers may reflect either a very strict division of labour or the operation of taboos on speech (usually the speech of women). There are societies, for instance, where if women want to use words that sound similar to the names of tabooed male relatives, they must resort to euphemism and circumlocution.

The case of English

In English, we tend to find sex-preferential rather than sex-exclusive markers. The main difference identified in sociolinguistic surveys on both sides of the Atlantic is that women's speech in every socioeconomic class deviates less from the prestige standard than men's. This applies both to grammatical form and to pronunciation.

Obviously, a difference of this type does not lend itself to explanations from either history or occupation, and several other reasons for it have therefore been advanced, based on supposed characteristics of females. Four in particular are very common: conservatism (whereas men innovate, women stick to the traditional standard forms); social climbing (women are more sensitive than men to the social meaning of speech, and imitate prestige usage in order to elevate their social status); feminine identity (it is feminine to 'talk like a lady', i.e. like a middle-class speaker) and covert prestige (in fact, non-standard speech is considered a sign of masculinity, and males cultivate it, so that no real prestige attaches to the more standard speech of women).

These four explanations of why women's speech deviates less from the prestige standard beg a number of questions and raise a number of problems. It seems necessary to ask, for instance, whether they are adequate accounts of the observed facts; whether they embody covert value-judgements downgrading women, and whether any alternative explanations are possible.

It is immediately obvious that the four proposals are not all compatible with each other. For example, women could not be both conservatives who did *not* innovate, and social climbers who sought to elevate their status by imitating prestige usage. Moreover, either of these possibilities – conservatism or social climbing – would require further explanation. Why are women more conservative than men? Or alternatively, why are they more aware than men of social norms, and more ambitious/conformist in their attitudes?

Certain other puzzles arise in relation to women's conservatism. Linguists who claim that women are conservative must believe this is a consequence of femininity itself, rather than subordination: for the groups most associated with the direction of linguistic change (i.e. the most innovative groups) are specifically subordinate groups, like the young and the lower middle class, who are said to suffer from linguistic 'insecurity'. Labov, the New York City researcher, has pointed to lower middle-class women in particular as trend-setters. Their pattern of style-shift (changing the way they talk when they become aware of it in more formal situations) suggests they are very sensitive to prestige markers in speech, and Labov speculates that they are in an especially good position to disseminate changes, since they can pass them on to their children. This supports the 'social climbing' theory rather than female conservatism. Moreover, cross-cultural evidence suggests that conservatism is not a universally feminine trait. In some patriarchal peasant societies, Madagascar for instance, it is women whose use of language breaks traditional rules.

The link between prestige usage and perceived femininity is more promising. It is anecdotally attested in many communities where one finds agreement that certain speech styles are all right for boys, but you wouldn't want your daughter/sister/girlfriend talking like that. 'Like that' in this context means swearing and coarseness, but also, and especially, pronunciation. A strong regional accent, which in England signifies either membership of or sympathy with the working class, is more acceptable in men than in women. This ties in with the idea of 'covert prestige' invented by the Norwich researcher, Peter Trudgill. Trudgill found that working-class speakers actually valued non-standard speech as a symbol of masculinity, and he advocated that we should reverse our class-based notion of prestige for these speakers to take account of the truism that anything men do is automatically more prestigious than anything women do. In Trudgill's opinion, for most working class speakers the prestige of standard English is overridden by the need to identify as a real man.[15]

If it is true that non-standard speech connotes masculinity, then we would expect to find femininity being constructed in deliberate opposition, as it is in so many other areas. This would explain the strong pressure put on women to talk like ladies, and the contempt reserved for those who intrude on the realm of the masculine with their strong regional accents.

VALUE JUDGEMENTS

It is very noticeable that the most popular explanations of women's more standard speech, conservatism and social climbing, are also very sexist, couching the qualities predicated of all women (itself a sexist strategy) in terms which downgrade them relative to men.

For instance, take the idea that men are innovative and women conservative. In our culture, innovation is valued, so this proposition implicitly praises the behaviour of men: the same thing could have been expressed as women's respect for tradition and men's cavalier disregard for it. In Madagascar, where things are exactly the other way around and it is men who are conservative, this is precisely how it is expressed. Men are guardians of a revered tradition, women the upstarts who can't be trusted to speak well in public. 'The use of direct speech, such as that of women, is associated with a loss of tradition.'[16] Unsurprisingly, 'Men alone are considered to be able speech-makers'.[17] The notion of covert prestige is also pervaded with sexism, though it does have the virtue of recording a prejudice that really exists. Trudgill is really saying that where women's language has to be defined as more prestigious than men's we should change the definition of prestige. The Madagascar example shows he is right: societies frame their definitions of prestige in accordance with the social and sexual hierarchy.

One possibility which is rarely addressed by linguists is that the finding itself, that women deviate less from the prestige standard, may be partly an artefact of the methodology used. Two aspects of sociolinguistic methodology particularly invite a critique.

The first of these is stratification. Sociolinguistic surveys are obviously dependent on some kind of stratifying procedure to determine which speakers belong to which socioeconomic class, and the criteria are normally occupational – unskilled versus skilled manual work, white collar versus professional. But these criteria are not usually applied to married women. Because the family is taken as the unit of stratification, and the key to the family's status is the occupation of its 'Head', married women are usually assigned to classes on the basis of their husband's occupation.

It has been argued by the feminist sociologist Christine Delphy that this stratification procedure is a grave defect, and persists only because it succeeds in obscuring essential mechanisms of patriarchy.[18] It places men and women in the same class and thus affirms their parity, yet this parity, which is only a by-product of marriage in any case, conceals the economic dependence of wives on their husbands.

Delphy's critique has certain implications for the sociolinguist. Although the distortion may not be very great, it is possible that stratification methods which assign women to classes according to their husbands' occupation distort the picture. The differences between men and women may partly reflect the fact that if one used other criteria for the stratification – educational attainment for instance – married couples might not turn out to be parallel at all.

The other problematic area is accommodation to the interviewer. It is well known that people speak differently in more and less formal situations. In a formal situation like an interview they will use a more standard variety than when they are not monitoring their behaviour so carefully. The style produced in casual situations is known as the 'vernacular', and contains fewest prestige features. Sociolinguists are more interested in this style than in any other, but it is extremely hard to collect samples of.

Being interviewed in a sociolinguistic survey is not a casual situation, and for most speakers the interviewer will be a social superior rather than a peer with whom the vernacular might be used. Therefore researchers have difficulty in eliciting anything less formal than an interview style.

Labov, the New York researcher, used a number of strategies to try and elicit the vernacular. He asked questions about traumatic experiences in the hope that informants would get carried away and forget to monitor their speech. He recorded incidental talk with family members who did not know the tape was running. And when he studied the language of Harlem gangs, he used a young, black fieldworker, since he knew the black vernacular was unlikely to be used with a white middle-class academic.

Since Labov, it has been considered desirable to minimise social distance between subject and interviewer (in a number of surveys local interviewers were used). Yet no one has extended this precaution to gender, or investigated whether it makes any difference. In talking to men, it could be argued, women are

always talking to their superordinates, and perhaps the
vernacular they might use with each other is just very seldom
elicited.

It should be clear by now that while sociolinguistic surveys
produce rather more reliable findings than the anecdotal
tradition, the explanations they put forward to account for those
findings have a tendency to be ad hoc and sexist. How then do
feminists reinterpret the findings of sex difference studies? Can
we be sure sex-linked variation has any political significance at
all?

DIFFERENCE AND DOMINANCE: THE IMPLICATIONS OF LINGUISTIC VARIATION

For some linguists, the varieties spoken by men and women are
rather like regional dialects or age-linked varieties: they reflect
the differing socialisation of women, the fact that women interact
more with each other than with men, and the existence of
particular feminine identities or gender roles which generate their
own norms of speaking and behaving. This 'subcultural' view of
sex difference (espoused for instance by Kramarae,[19] and Maltz
and Borker,[20]) may or may not stress the position of female
subcultures in the power hierarchy. Some commentators point
out that women are not entirely free to develop their own
subcultural norms, because the femininity they are socialised into
and seek to express is to a large extent male-defined, while others
give the impression that power is merely an extraneous factor
grafted on to the subcultural ecology.

Other linguists, however, see a much more direct link between
the position of women in particular societies and the actual
differences between their speech and men's. Sex differences for
them must be given a primarily political explanation, and the
speech style forced upon women must be shown as inherently
oppressive.

Proponents of this view (e.g. Lakoff)[21] describe female speech
as a function of women's linguistic insecurity, which is ultimately
a reflection of their social marginality and need to be seen as
deferring to male norms. The phonetician Caroline Henton, for
instance, sees this insecurity as the key to understanding

differences which on the face on it have no obvious relation to oppression at all: differences in the pitch and vowel-quality of women and men that are either too great or of the wrong kind to be explained by any sex difference in vocal-tract anatomy.[22]

Henton's explanation is that women perceive a norm which they then overshoot in their production of vowels. She sees the fact that pitch and vowel quality are not under conscious control as very important, since it indicates how deep the insecurity goes; she also points out that since these differences are instrumentally measurable, they cannot be the misreported products of stereotypes held either by the informant or the analyst.

Although systematic non-innate differences in something so fundamental as vowel-quality do indeed call for an explanation, and that explanation is unlikely to have anything to do with conscious motives and attitudes, no amount of instrumental measuring can tell us what the explanation *is*. Henton's account is more acceptable to feminists, and indeed to scientists, than the folkphonetics of Swift, but the problem of what causes or motivates the differences remains.

But is this the crucial problem in the politics of linguistic sex difference? It may be interesting to discover the origins and the meaning of differences but difference itself is not the key to women's oppression through language. The key is value-judgement; the way difference is perceived, the consequences it has. In looking at these things we need make no distinction between real differences and folklinguistic stereotypes: indeed we can bring them together to produce an integrated account of what sex differences mean in our society.

We may consider, for instance, the fact that women are sometimes discriminated against ostensibly because of the way they speak. In some jobs they must be more 'well-spoken' than a man would have to be; in others, especially broadcasting jobs, they may be told that female voices are too 'tinny' or 'high' and that they 'lack authority'. It has even been suggested that the reluctance of juries to believe women in court is partly because their range of intonational and pitch contrasts (which is greater than men's) suggests hysteria.

Yet it would be native to suppose these complaints have any real linguistic substance. Some of the unpleasant quality of women's broadcast voices (supposing it exists) may be due to filters on recording equipment which turn up the treble (as male voices require) rather than the bass. Audio equipment was not designed for women. But pleasantness to a large extent resides in the ear of the listener, and predictably enough, there is widespread prejudice against women's voices.

As for 'hysterical' and 'lacking in authority', it is inconceivable that these judgements can ultimately have anything to do with pitch. If men talked in higher voices than women, low voices would be said to lack authority. The point is that in our culture, anything that marks a speaker out as female becomes a cause for complaint and a proof of inferiority.

Linguistic sex-differences act simply as a badge of femaleness, and are valued negatively quite irrespective of their substance. Explaining that women's high pitch is learned/can be authoritative/is really very pleasing to the ear will have no effect on the irrational process by which everything 'female' is pejorated, whether it actually reflects women's behaviour or not.

A particularly inept sociolinguistic study reported in Smith 1979 will serve as an illustration.[23] An experiment was set up to investigate whether, in a courtroom, male and female speech styles would be found equally credible by a jury. Two versions of the same narrative were proposed, one a 'male' version using the pronunciation, tone of voice and grammar supposedly typical of men, and the other a 'female' version similarly treated. The female version was judged less credible even when delivered by a carefully trained man, and the experimenters therefore concluded that the lack of credibility lay in the language and not the speaker.

What they overlooked, however, was simply that the 'female' version did not reflect women's actual speech style, but only the stereotyped style people ascribe to them. It may well have failed to reflect any real speaker's style, and its lack of credibility could have been predicted from that alone.

We have already examined the tendency of feminists to make unwarranted statements about female speech style, and to believe in simplistic stereotypes. It appears that in addition they tend to accept the normal valuations of various linguistic features as signs of powerlessness, deference and so on, concluding that men have forced women to learn an inherently powerless speech style which reinforces their actual powerlessness. The truth is that although women may be forced to learn a style of speaking that different iates them from men and identifies them as women, the labels which condemn this style embody not obvious truths but value judgements which would be applied to anything female. As the saying goes, 'a woman's place is in the wrong', and this is as true of language as it is of anything else.

Let us take the much argued case of tag-questions as an example for discussion. Many feminists are familiar with Lakoff's assertion that the tag-question is characteristic of female speech because it is 'approval-seeking', half-way between a statement and a question. It moderates the offensiveness of a woman's telling a man something straight out.

In fact, it turned out on investigation that women's attachment to the tag-question could not be confirmed empirically. Dubois and Crouch found men using it rather more.[24] Dale Spender was very concerned about this finding, and tried to explain it away: she pointed out that since it is hard to tell tentative tags (that'll be all right, won't it?) from forceful ones (don't do that again, will you?) maybe women used the tentative ones and men the forceful ones. Spender also observed that no one tried to explain the new finding that men used tag-questions more, by saying they were seeking approval.[25]

In fact, we can surely account for the second point in terms of what the first implies, and the account is a revealing one. Out of context, it simply is not possible to state once and for all what a tag-question means. It could be tentativeness, forcefulness, checking information (the concert starts at eight, doesn't it?) patronising someone (that can't be the case, can it?) and any number of other things. Whatever function we ascribe to tag-questions or any other grammatical form, can only be a rationalisation after the event. If that is true, it is not surprising that when men are found using tag-questions the rationalisation does not include approval-seeking. The cultural stereotype of men tells us they do not need to seek approval.

Lakoff was not, as Spender implies, attempting to prove that women's speech lacked effectiveness, but that it contained tangible evidence of their need, which she took for granted, not to be seen as over-assertive by men. The mistake lies in equating linguistic forms with extra-linguistic needs in a one-to-one correspondence: tag-questions do not always express a need for approval, and the need for approval is not always expressed by tag-questions.

The argument here can be summarized in three points.

1.   Women do not use more tag-questions than men.
2.   Even if they did, it would not necessarily mean they were seeking approval, since tag-questions have a range of uses.
3.   In any case, women's use of tag-questions will always be explained differently from men's, since it is cultural sex stereotypes which determine the explanation of linguistic phenomena, rather than the nature of the phenomena themselves.

In this chapter I have tried to show why paying attention to the metalinguistic (what people say about talk and how they analyse it) is a crucial part of understanding the significance of sex-difference and the ways in which linguists have dealt with it. In Chapter 4 I propose to look at a different aspect of metalinguistic politics: the way in which grammarians and linguists have projected a male/female dichotomy on to the languages of the world, and their attempts to use grammar as a tactical weapon in the battle of the sexes.

4 False Dichotomies: Grammar and Sexual Polarity

> Theoretically, it is possible
> to classify any phenomenon as
> male or female.
>
> *Marielouise Janssen-Jurreit*

> Thought has always worked by
> opposition,
> Speech/Writing,
> High/Low . . .
> Does this mean something? Is
> the fact that logocentrism subjects
> all thought — all of the
> concepts, the codes, the values —
> to a two-term system, related to
> 'the' couple man/woman?
>
> *Hélène Cixous*

Yin and yang; animus and anima; as the epigraphs to this chapter point out, a tendency to classify the universe by an opposition of male and female principles recurs in patriarchal thinking. But is the opposition such a true and fundamental one? A basic insight produced by the feminist theory of this century (we owe it to Simone de Beauvoir[1] and it has been developed by Luce Irigaray)[2] is that women in patriarchy are constructed as the Other — as whatever men are not. If man is active, woman is passive; if he has the phallus, she simply lacks it. Femininity is masculinity inverted.

Irigaray points out the reductive inaccuracy of this concept when applied, say, to female sexuality. Women are different from men, but not opposite to them, and the binary oppositions which locate them at one end of a male/female polarity are artificial, reflecting both the exclusion of women from the making of what counts as knowledge (philosophy and science, for instance) and the dominance of one particular sort of science. For as Jane Gallop observes, in a scientific model 'otherness is suppressed to preserve the theory's consistency. Theory's authority is guaranteed by its consistency.'[3]

This chapter is about the projection of the male/female opposition on to language and especially on to the analytic construct, grammar. I want to consider whether it is a natural or reasonable practice: whether it has ill effects for women: how feminists have responded to it and whether their criticism is well-founded.

The binary opposition has a special status in linguistics. The reader will recall that Saussure placed great stress on contrast as a principle of linguistic structure, and that he drew a number of binary distinctions himself (langue/parole, synchronic/diachronic, syntagmatic/paradigmatic). Since Saussure, many other linguists have found the two-way contrast useful in their analyses of linguistic systems from phonology upwards, and it has become institutionalised. Students learn early to look for binary oppositions rather than, say, three-term contrasts, in language, and may even be told what some theorists maintain, that to do so is a universal property of the human mind. After all, why should these contrasts keep turning up if they are not somehow 'natural'?

It is useful to separate out the two questions which arise from this account. The first is whether we should reify (treat as a thing) the binary opposition as so many writers seem to do. Do oppositions exist in the language to be *discovered* by linguistic science, or are they *invented* as a handy way of analysing language? In other words, is the binary opposition principle a claim about linguistic structure or a claim about what analytic strategies most naturally come to the linguist?

The second is a nature/nurture question. If there really is a tendency to think in opposites, whether or not it reflects the existence of those oppositions in the world, is this tendency innate in the human mind, or is it inculcated by upbringing and education? When we look at the reasons why linguists have asserted that the binary distinction is innate, they seem far from convincing. The first reason is that since the binary opposition is basic to language, this must reflect a property of the mind: which is surely circular, as it takes for granted the very point (that languages really are organised around two-way contrasts) which is at issue. The second reason derives from information theory, a subject centred on studying the transmission of messages. In information theory, a maximally efficient communication system employs two-way contrasts because they are easy to process, involving only one decision, whether an item is 'x or not-x'. But however useful this idea may be when applied to machine languages, it is not an adequate account of human communication. In any case, linguistics habitually equates very different sorts of opposition. There are choices in language that fit the 'x or not-x' pattern, but there are others that do not. This is especially obvious when we analyse languages at the level of semantics (meaning).

The semantic model most obviously dependent on binary oppositions is called componential analysis. The aim of it is to reduce the meaning of a word to a series of supposedly primitive features for which it has either a plus or a minus value. So the word *animal*, for instance, would be given the features + animate and − human. Some exponents of this theory believe that the primitive features are innate, and that making binary classifications of this type is an important element in human cognition.[4]

It is clear that when we assign features like animateness and humanness the choice is an either/or one (although it is interesting to speculate on how speakers would assign intelligent robots). But consider another pair of opposites, *old* and *young*. Componential analysis would handle them with one feature, ± old. But although they are dictionary antonyms, the qualities they denote are not really opposed: rather, they are on a continuum. Just because a middle-aged person is not young (− young) she is not necessarily old.

The linguist who equates oppositions where yes and no cover all the possibilities with those where degree must be distinguished has been fooled by the language. Because she knows (has learned, in fact: most children do a lot of formal learning of antonyms) the words are 'opposites', she does not bother to check that their meanings are.

The male/female opposition obviously does not fall into this category, since anatomically speaking, every animate being must be either male or female. But it is not at all obvious that the feature ± male captures any awareness of this on the part of a speaker when she defines various words. In other words, do the creatures either side of the gender division have opposite qualities that are relevant to people's conceptualisation of them, and to their use of words?

PLUS AND MINUS MALE: NEGATIVE SEMANTIC SPACE

In *Man Made Language*, Dale Spender takes issue with the componential analysts and claims that their practices show the relegation of women to a 'negative semantic space' in the English language. The practice she cites is the common way of representing words with a female component in their meaning, such as *girl* and *wife*, not as + female but as − male.

Spender rightly remarks that this is sexist (after all, it is equally correct to represent males as − female; all that matters is that one duality should define all the possibilities and that everything should have either a plus or a minus value in respect of it). But she seems to feel that the bias is not only in the analyst but actually in the language, implying that women are classified by speakers of English as the negative of men. 'One of our fundamental rules for making sense of the...world is...that the male represents the positive while the female, necessarily then, represents the negative.'[5] It is possible to adduce a good deal of evidence in support of this claim, and arguably the practices of componential analysts constitute just such evidence. But we are on shakier ground if we claim it is a rule of language itself that female terms have a negative meaning. This is to reify mere (though sexist) terminology. It is woolly thinking to imagine that linguistics has discovered a Law instead of acknowledging that − male is a theoretical invention reflecting the bias of its creators.

There is no claim implicit in the use of − male that male is the norm and female the exception. It does not matter which end of a polarity is + and which −, though of course the choice reflects our conventional priorities (which are not, or not only, linguistic). To say that the language embodies value judgements based on these plus and minus categories is a theoretical vulgarity even the most chauvinist linguist would repudiate.

The argument which is germane here is one we have already touched on: how accurate is it, both objectively and as a representation of lay knowledge/belief, to construct a binary opposition between male and female built into the meaning of words? Might this not be a false dichotomy which persists, and not only in language, because of the amount of political energy which has been invested in it?

Yet it might be said that although the dichotomy is an over-simplification, the structure of language forces it upon us. Language's natural binarity predisposed us to pair words like male and female and to treat them as opposites. The theme of this chapter is the way in which grammar and its practitioners have fooled us – sometimes deliberately – by convincing us that artificial and theoretical biases are really inherent in the language. To the extent that grammar does this, it actually alters the way we look at the world, and feminists must expose the ideological task it is carrying out. Opposites are a good place to start, since it is not hard to see they are a blatant example of 'fixing'.

Readers will probably recall learning at school the concept of a lexical opposite and a list of pairs exemplifying it. It would be very strange if these pairs were innate in anyone's mind, since they are extraordinarily conventional, heterogeneous and in many cases opaque. Who as a child could have said why *black* and *white* are opposites? *Day* and *night*, though more obvious, are quite different, and sometimes (e.g. in the context of clothes) *evening* is the opposite of *day*. There are polar opposites like *North* and *South*, and pseudo-opposites like *long/short*. The principle of duality, rather than being innate, has to be etched on the conceptual apparatus of the child.

Lexical antonyms, then, cannot be generated from a single principle, do not hold good from context to context and vary from culture to culture. Therefore it is an exercise in futility to use them as representations of what people know about word-meaning, or to claim they are innate. The emphasis placed on *learning* antonyms suggests that the urge to dichotomise is secondary indoctrination rather than native habit, typical not so much of ordinary talk but of the systems our societies have to teach us, of logic and dialectic. And even if dichotomy were a strong tendency in human thinking, it would hardly follow that particular pairs were innate. It seems unlikely, also, that dichotomised thinking is engendered by language and the binary nature of linguistic meaning, because models like componential analysis which are based on binary choices are very bad at representing what people know about the differences between related words. Simple 'x/not-x' choices are very rarely appropriate.   .

So it seems pointless for feminists to pursue the sexism of componential analysis: rather, they should dismiss it, and its system of oppositions, as a fundamentally wrong account of meaning. The male/female opposition itself, of course, remains of cultural and political interest to feminists. As Hélène Cixous points out, it is felt in many societies to be the fundamental dichotomy: but the explanation lies mostly outside linguistics, reflecting a very general and conscious patriarchal policy of constructing a sexual dichotomy in every area of human experience.

THE CASE OF GENDER: GRAMMAR AND SEXIST IDEOLOGY

Perhaps the oldest and most familiar example of a male/female dichotomy in language is the grammatical category of gender. Gender has a long history of provoking controversy among grammarians, philosophers, philologists and social theorists: not surprisingly, it is often discussed by feminists in the contemporary debate about sexism in language.

Yet despite centuries of argument, the issues (linguistic and political) that gender raises seem to have been confused rather than resolved with every fresh attempt at explication. What follows here is an attempt to clarify the notion of gender and to deal with the historical and current controversies from a feminist point of view. I particularly want to demonstrate that the supposedly objective intellectual pronouncements of traditional grammarians and linguistic scientists alike have always participated in, and been coloured by, the general ideology of male superiority and sexual difference.

What is gender?

Like a lot of our traditional grammatical terms, *gender* originated in the linguistic scholarship of Greece. It is usually credited to the sophist Protagoras. The word itself is derived from a word meaning 'class' or 'kind' and was used to divide Greek nouns into three classes, traditionally labelled masculine, feminine and neuter.

Greek is one of the many languages which possess what is known as grammatical gender. The three-way classification masculine/feminine/neuter does not reflect any common-sense division of word meanings into male, female and inanimate, but rather the fact that nouns can behave in three different ways when it comes to the agreement of adjectives, the choice of article, replacement by a pronoun and inflectional patterns (word endings). Masculine, feminine and neuter are merely labels for formal properties of words, and do not reflect word meaning at all (thus in German, the word for a girl is neuter, while that for a turnip is feminine).

Not all languages exhibit this kind of noun classification. Some, like Chinese, have nothing we could label gender at all, whereas others, like the African Bantu languages, have more than three types. English is an example of a further type, usually called *natural gender*. What this means is that only those words which refer to something with a biological sex can be masculine or feminine. The vast majority of words will be neither (or, if they refer to people, will have the ability to be both, which is called *common gender*: words like *friend* and *driver* have common gender). It is easy to see why English speakers regard this arrangement as natural: it appears to have its roots in common-sense reality, whereas the foreign habit of assigning a gender to anything from a turnip to a sideboard strikes us as nothing more than a bizarre morphological whim.

Feminists, contemplating such usages as 'Man is unique among the apes in that he grows a long beard, and it is to this that he owes his superior intelligence'[6] have pointed out that English gender is natural only if you are a man. This observation marks a step in the right direction: some aspects of, say, pronoun replacement (e.g. that ships and cars are *she*) cry out for a cultural rather than nature/grammar explanation. But what is really needed is a critique of these notions subsumed under the heading of gender. What does gender have to do with sex, and why do linguists work hard at obfuscating that issue? How natural is natural gender, how common is common gender and how grammatical is grammatical gender?

Grammatical gender

Grammatical gender has inspired innumerable articles and speculations from the ancient Greeks to the modern linguists, but it seems not to have preoccupied English-speaking feminists (Dale Spender, for instance, dismisses it in two sentences as a preamble to her remarks on English gender). It is clear, however, that grammatical gender is a feminist issue, if only because remarks on its origin and nature have so frequently been part of male arguments against women's rights. The German feminist Marielouise Janssen-Jurreit sums up a long historical debate like this: 'For two thousand years there has been an unresolved question: whether word endings of nouns and pronouns, as well as articles, are an extension of the qualities regarded as male or female.'[7] For a number of reasons, contemporary linguists reject the idea that there is any necessary connection between grammatical gender and sex. Lyons is typical in asserting that while gender does reflect some natural semantic classification of the world, by shape, colour or texture, for example, the crucial factor is 'not necessarily sex'.[8] But Janssen-Jurreit's survey of the debate makes it quite clear that previous scholars, from the Greek sophists to the nineteenth-century philologists, would not have agreed with Lyons. On the contrary, it seems to have been generally believed that grammatical gender is assigned on the basis of natural sex difference, and clear exceptions to this rule were thought aberrant, in need of explanation and possibly even reform.

Thus Protagoras, the pioneer of the gender concept, made various attempts at linguistic reform, claiming that gender should be assigned on some logical and consistent basis. For this he was ridiculed by Aristophanes, and the attempt was not a success. Nevertheless, the idea behind it persisted. The Germanic philologist Grimm, for instance, addressed the question of what abstract criteria determine the gender of a word. Grimm's theory was that grammatical gender is a later stage of natural gender, a more advanced form, as it were, of the common-sense classification which takes into account only biological sex. According to this theory, languages develop grammatical gender when their speakers pass from mere recognition of male and female creatures to the postulation of abstract male and female principles in whose terms everything and anything could be classified. Grimm spelt out exactly which qualities went with which gender. He felt (the girl and the turnip notwithstanding) these qualities were present in the meanings of words: 'The masculine means the earlier, larger, firmer, more inflexible, swift, active, mobile, productive; the feminine the later, smaller, smoother, the more still, suffering, receptive.'[9]

Having used stereotypes of male and female qualities to explain grammatical gender, writers in some cases turned to gender for guidance on the 'natural' attributes of womankind. According to Janssen-Jurreit, even pro-feminist Theodor Hippel believed women were irrational on the grounds that the German word for reason is masculine in gender. (Presumably Hippel would have allowed that in France, where the word for reason is feminine, the men are irrational!) That this type of argument could even be proposed demonstrates the close correspondence which was taken for granted between grammatical gender distinctions and sex differences.

Another point which was taken for granted was the relative value of the three genders (masculine, feminine, neuter) and it is clear that some communities in their use of language exploit this ranking to encode the inferiority of women, or of some women relative to others. In Konkani, an Indian language, women of low status because of youth or widowhood are referred to by neuter pronouns, only married women getting the courtesy of the feminine.[10] We may link this phenomenon with the frequently attested reluctance of successful French and German women to accept titles such as 'Stadtssekretärin' which have been feminised, on the grounds that these downgrade them: '. . . the successful Madame prefers to be le Docteur, le Professeur, l'Ambassadeur and le Philosophe, even with the succeeding *il* which is required in formal texts.'[11] Whatever the origin of grammatical gender, it cannot be true that it has nothing to do with sex, since a long lay and linguistic tradition that it *is* a matter of sex clearly allows it to be pressed into service as a marker of patriarchal values and relations.

Natural gender

So far our interest has focused on the claim that grammatical gender is actually natural, reflecting immutable realities of sex difference. Recently, however, this claim has been turned on its head in an exactly symmetrical fashion, as English-speaking linguists attempt to deny that 'natural' gender has anything to do with the realities of a sexist society.

The classic statement of this position comes from the linguistics faculty at Harvard University. When theology students objected to the use of male pronouns to refer to God, seventeen members of the faculty wrote to the *Harvard Crimson* with the following statement about what they wittily dubbed 'pronoun envy'.

> Many of the grammatical and lexical oppositions in a language are not between equal members of a pair, but between two entities one of which is more marked than the other.... For people and pronouns in English the masculine is unmarked and hence is used as a neutral or unspecified term.... The fact that the masculine is unmarked in English (or that the feminine is unmarked in the language of the Tunica Indians) is simply a feature of grammar.[12]

It is difficult to imagine why these distinguished academics would have thrown their considerable intellectual weight behind such a statement unless they found the issue threatening. Even without the ominous noises of axe-grinding, however, it would be necessary to dismiss the learned gentlemen for the essential incoherence of their argument.

Marking theory is the newest red herring in the gender debate. Even feminist scholars like Dubois and Crouch fall under its technical spell, and rather sneeringly remark of their non-linguist sisters,

> they may be forgiven for failing to understand the theory of marking, which explains that *he* can be unmarked for sex in certain contexts but marked for it in others. Even now, statements about 'the essential absurdity of using the same symbols for all the human race in one breath and for only half of it in the next' betray ignorance of this principle widely operative in languages.[13]

It is therefore worth looking at marking theory and at its application to gender. Marking – or the use of the terms *marked* and *unmarked* – implies that linguistic elements are like the animals on Orwell's farm: some are more equal than others. Since the rise of a linguistics centrally concerned with universals, the marking claim usually involves asserting that some elements will always be found earlier or more frequently than others. An example is that the vowel /u/ (as in *boot*) turns up in the languages of the world more often that /y/ (as in French *lune*). Any language that has /y/ will also have /u/, whereas the reverse is not true.

It is hard to see how this claim could apply to gender, even if we allow it is a real category and not a linguist's construct. For some languages have the masculine unmarked, others like Tunica the feminine. The genders do not form a hierarchy across languages as /u/ and /y/ are said to do. So the claim about gender-marking must be language specific. What, in that case, does it imply?

By looking at various precedents for the use of *marked* and *unmarked* in linguistic analysis, it can be seen that linguists commonly make use of three criteria to justify labelling some variant unmarked relative to other marked variants. The first of these is precisely the ability to be used generically, in a way that includes or subsumes marked variants. But in the case of gender this is an entirely circular claim: *he* is unmarked because it is generic, but it is generic because it is unmarked. We are no further on with the explanation. What factors determine that something can be used generically, and are they entirely linguistic?

The second criterion for labelling something unmarked is relative neutrality of meaning. But in the case of gender what can this be but a social value judgement? To whom does *he* sound more neutral than *she*, and why?

Thirdly, we have the criterion of frequency of occurrence. If something is found more frequently than its alternants, linguists are liable to say it is unmarked by comparison with them.

It is at this point that we should recall the grammar book dictum that English gender is not grammatical but natural, that is, dictated by semantic rather than formal characteristics of words. If this account is correct (and there is no reason to suppose that English has gender in the same way French and German have it, nor that Dubois and Crouch are unaware of this) we have no business explaining the relative frequency of masculine and feminine pronouns in terms of universal, or even arbitrary, grammatical rules. If gender is fixed extra-linguistically by sex-reference, then the occurrence of more masculine than feminine pronouns, the generic, neutral and unspecified male, requires an extra-linguistic justification too.

And the actual explanation delivers the *coup de grâce* to the Harvard faculty. One of the most thoroughly documented phenomena in feminist research has been the rise of sexist practices in prescriptive grammar, and it is this which turns out to be at the bottom of unmarked *he*. Since at least 1553, when one Thomas Wilson asserted the precedence of masculine nouns and pronouns, grammarians have been attempting to eliminate the tendency still present in ordinary speech to use *they* as a singular for generic or unspecified referents (as in 'you can't blame a person if they get angry about sexist grammar'). John Kirkby's *Eighty Eight Grammatical Rules* of 1746 stated that the masculine is more comprehensive than the feminine, and this view found its way into the statute books by 1850, when *he* was held legally to stand for *she* (though this kind of formulation always leaves open the possibility that women will be excluded from the definition, for instance when they claim the rights of a *person* or *citizen*).

In all these grammatical treatises (which are given a full treatment by Ann Bodine)[14] there was an appeal not to the laws of language but to those of nature: the generic masculine was said to have the virtues of 'naturalness' and 'propriety'. And while generic *they* has never been eradicated from speech, it has been stigmatised as non-standard, incorrect and unacceptable in writing.

Unmarked *he* is indeed a feature of grammar – of prescriptive grammar, reinforced by male grammarians for avowedly ideological reasons. The whole affair illustrates the ill-effects of pseudo-scientific linguistics: for if the Harvard faculty had applied scholarship and sought out the historical and cultural practices determining English gender rules, they would not have made the mistake of reifying their terms.

Common gender

The phenomenon of common gender – where a noun can be either masculine or feminine – is found in both grammatical and natural gender languages. In English, for instance, *person*, *consumer* and *teacher* have common gender, while in French *enfant* and *personne*, though grammatically masculine and feminine respectively, require adjectives, etc. to agree on the basis of sex-reference. But how common is common gender? Although it is obvious that words like *person* are capable of either a masculine or a feminine interpretation depending on the contexts, there are some respects in which common gender nouns exhibit a sexual asymmetry.

A random foray into any newspaper will eventually reveal usages like the following: 'FOURTEEN SURVIVORS, THREE OF THEM WOMEN ...', or 'PEOPLE ARE MUCH MORE LIKELY TO BE INFLUENCED BY THEIR WIVES THAN BY OPINION POLLS.' It will never reveal, on the other hand, 'FOURTEEN SURVIVORS, THREE OF THEM MEN ...', or 'PEOPLE ARE MUCH MORE LIKELY TO BE INFLUENCED BY THEIR HUSBANDS THAN BY OPINION POLLS.'

Is the common gender basically masculine then? It is not, of course, impossible to say 'my grandmother is a survivor of two world wars' or 'Marianne and Elinor are very strange people'. But whereas it is possible, and in some cases apparently obligatory, to make a special case of women, this is not possible when one is talking about men.

Maria Black and Rosalind Coward, in an article criticising Dale Spender, argue that this phenomenon derives from a more general 'discursive practice' within our culture, whereby men have available to represent them a discourse of general human-ness, as well as a discourse of masculine sexuality, while women have available to them only one discourse in which their sexuality is paramount.[15] Men may efface their masculinity, but femininity can never be effaced. This produces the effect that women are an exception to the male norm.

The problem for feminists is to make men confront and take responsibility for their sexuality, as women must theirs. For Black and Coward, gender asymmetries are not the product of gender rules in language, but of historically evolved ways of representing things, or cultural discourses as they are termed, which define the nature and limits of femininity and masculinity. One attacks these discourses primarily by becoming aware of them and by developing rival discourses (ways of representing) that people will eventually incorporate into their own method of dealing with reality.

A rather more banal explanation of gender anomalies is simply that many speakers using words like *friend* on particular occasions do not 'have women in mind'. Since they are not thinking of females they have no need to select a form appropriate to talking about females. Only the pseudo-generic nature of most words and the non-specificity of most contexts fool us into imagining that most utterances do not explicitly exclude women.

Whether or not one agrees with Black and Coward, gender is evidently a candidate for serious re-examination by feminists. It is clear that our ideas about gender and sex affect the way the category is used in lay language, and the way it is analysed by linguists. Some combination of the linguistic and the metalinguistic produces the kind of regularity Black and Coward call a 'discourse': and this regularity cannot be understood in linguistic terms alone.

All of this gives the lie to the linguist's assertion that gender and sex have nothing to do with each other. Analyses of gender are coloured by ideas about sex, and may be invoked in defence of ideas about sex. The repeated assertion that these gender phenomena are just part of the language, open only to a technical and apolitical explanation, simply serves to obscure the ideological and prescriptive nature of what grammarians do.

It is in general true that linguists shy away from the ideological implications of their analyses, since to admit these exist is to question the objectivity of science, or else the scientific status of linguistics itself. One of their methods for distancing themselves from political questions is the maintenance of theoretical fictions like *langue*, through which they are reassured that they are dealing with a system and not with the willed acts of speakers who inhabit the real world of social and power relations (thus we get the absurdity of the Harvard faculty, Dubois and Crouch *et al.* telling off speakers for wanting to make 'unnecessary' changes to the language, which is somehow seen as existing in its own right, independently of those who speak it). Another distancing strategy, as we have seen, is to ignore history.

But those of us who live in cultures with a long history of grammatical analysis cannot escape our history, and the fact is that our linguistic tradition is overwhelmingly a prescriptive one. Linguistic science does not begin on a tabula rasa, and just as we take traditional categories like *noun* and *tense* for our descriptive ools, so we have taken value judgements, prescriptions and myths. We must be prepared to examine linguistics for evidence of these and to work out their ideological implications, abandoning the idea that linguistic science can be unbiased. Grammar, and all other metalinguistic practices, cannot but be implicated in the oppression of women through patriarchal scholarship.

In this chapter we have been dealing with the sexism of grammar, attempting to separate out sexist attributes of *language* from the sexism projected on to language in the analytic responses of linguists. This has not always been easy, for metalinguistic practices sometimes turn out to have had considerable influence on the language itself. Bearing this in mind, we must now turn to the language itself', and to feminist ideas about linguistic reform.

5 Making Changes: Can We Decontaminate Sexist Language?

> At a deep level, changes in a language are threatening because they signal widespread changes in social mores.
>
> *Casey Miller and Kate Swift*

In the last chapter I looked at the sexism which is expressed in linguists' analyses of language, arguing that although its effects are not insignificant, this sexism lies essentially in the metasystem used by linguists rather than in the language itself. This chapter, however, concerns the sexism that feminists have found more of an everyday problem, since it is, so to speak, in the language itself. Most of all, this chapter concerns the theory and the practice of feminist linguistic reform.

The sexism of languages (as usual I shall be dealing primarily with English, but languages vary in the type and degree of sexism they display) is a subject invented and researched by feminists. The ideological framework they have used is simple and explicit: briefly, they start with the hypothesis that the lexicon, grammatical structure, etc. of a given language will contain features that exclude, insult or trivialise women, and they set out to identify the features in question. Some researchers posit underlying mechanisms of language change to account for asymmetries; others concentrate, as I did in the previous chapter, on prescriptive processes; some are interested in language as a sociological research tool, relating the changing definitions and uses of words to the differing forms of women's subordination; while others see it as their task to suggest changes that will eliminate or modify offensive forms.

Nor has this kind of 'verbal hygiene' been ignored. Many people who would never have thought about the matter just a few years ago believe now in the existence of 'sexist' and 'non-sexist' language, and expressions designated 'non-sexist' are turning up more and more in the usage of the media (an informal look at one day's newspapers, for instance, yielded an item on whether to replace generic *he* with *he or she* or *they*, a reference to *angry young men and women* and the word *spokeswoman* in a news report). Such awareness and willingness to change could not have come about without pressure from the women's movement.

Of course, many institutions and individuals – perhaps most – continue to use sexist language, and to defend its use. Their argument in doing so, however, has had to change. Instead of denying that a male bias exists, they pretend to object to change on the grounds that one should not tamper with grammar, that non-sexist forms are aesthetically inferior or even, as a last resort, that any willed change in language automatically ushers in 1984: 'The feminist attack on social crimes may be as legitimate as it was inevitable. But the attack on words is only another social crime – one against the means and the hope of communication.'[1] Once again, we have this notion of 'the language' as a hallowed institution whose traditions may not be queried. 'Words' may be attacked independently of their users, and this will be disastrous because it will render communication impossible. This picture of language as something external, independent and disinterested stops us asking whose language it is, whose traditions will be under attack if the conventions are changed. In this chapter, questions like these must be asked. It is not good enough to shrug our shoulders and say that male bias in usage is purely grammatical, and that therefore it does not matter.

Obviously, it does matter to feminists. Most of us are now thoroughly aware of the ways in which English insults, excludes and trivialises us (universal male pronouns, misogynist insult words, patriarchal personal names, trivialising suffixes for women in professions (*authoress*), *girl* used in contexts where *boy* would be unacceptable, words like *blonde* standing for the whole woman; etc., etc. and there is no need to rehearse them all over again in this book.

What does need to be discussed, though, is precisely *why* all this is so offensive. Is it just an unpleasant reminder that men see us either as scapegoats or as non-entities? Or is it positively harmful? Can we eliminate it through linguistic reform, and if so, should we?

Questions like these are especially interesting because feminists themselves do not agree on the answers. Although there may seem to be a consensus, the united front soon turns out to be an illusion: most feminists believe that sexist language is a bad thing, but they believe it for very different reasons. A particularly important difference is between those who consider language 'symptomatic' and those who consider it 'causal'.

The 'symptomatic' camp believe that sexist language is a symptom, a piece of rudeness which may well be quite unintentional. To the extent that it is the product of carelessness, ignorance and laziness, it can be cured by the linguistic reformer. The reformer works by (*a*) drawing the speaker's attention to the offending form, and to the underlying prejudice of which it is a symptom, and (*b*) suggesting a non-sexist alternative which the speaker, now made aware, can substitute for it.

Casey Miller and Kate Swift, authors of a comprehensive guide to non-sexist English, represent admirably the attitudes of the 'symptomatic' tendency.[2] For them, sexist language is an outdated excrescence which everyone but a few reactionaries would dearly love to be rid of; mere force of habit is the only thing that props it up. Since Miller and Swift subtitled their earlier book (*Words and Women*)[3] *New Language in New Times*, it seems they take the optimistic view that we are now living in a post-feminist world, and that their job is to help language catch up with society. Miller and Swift are strong on common sense and the 'facts':

> The public counts on those who disseminate factual in formation...to be as certain that what they tell us is as accurate as research and the conscientious use of language can make it. Only recently have we become aware that conventional English usage...obscures the actions, the contributions and sometimes even the very presence of women. Turning our backs on that insight is an option, of course, but it is an option like teaching children the world is flat.[4]

In other words, sexist language is to be condemned because it distorts the truth: once aware of this startling fact, right-thinking people will immediately proceed to self-criticism and reform. Purged of its prejudices, our language can indeed in the mouth of a 'conscientious' user, disseminate 'accurate' information.

I have no wish to belittle the important work of Miller and Swift, especially the detail in which they have worked out non-sexist alternative usages so that the most unimaginative writer, if well-meaning, can eliminate gross bias without gross inelegance. However, the stance of those who advocate non-sexist writing for the reasons Miller and Swift do is a theoretical reformism which leaves an enormous amount to be desired. One of the aims of this chapter is to produce a critique of theoretical reformism and of the assumptions about language that lie behind it.

Recently, the reformism of the 'symptomatic' camp has been explicitly criticised by other feminists. Dale Spender, for example, is a well-known supporter of the idea that language *causes* women's oppression rather than being a symptom of it. It is through a language that trivialises, excludes and insults us that we come to know our subordinate place in the world.

The 'causal' tendency has also extended the boundaries of what counts as sexism in language. Miller and Swift have a well-defined set of targets for reform: generic masculine pronouns, sex-differentiated job descriptions, *girl* used of adult women and so on. Dale Spender would insist that all words are sexist, since their meanings are fixed by men and embody male misogyny.

The question of whether linguistic sexism is a cause or an effect of women's oppression, and the problem of defining its boundaries, ultimately links up with the debate on language and reality, who controls language and who is alienated from it. I shall be examining that debate in detail in the next two chapters. In this chapter, however, I shall confine myself to the sorts of linguistic phenomena that worry both reformists and radicals: usages that are always and obviously sexist, and which might conceivably be the targets of organised reform campaigns. I particularly want to look at the ways in which feminists are hitting back at sexism informally, through private 'reclamation' and the coining of new terms, and institutionally, through demands for reforms in lexicographical and journalistic practice, etc.

Where sexism in language is concerned, feminists tend to proceed in two ways. When a problem area is identified, they are concerned both to draw out the political and historical implications of linguistic facts, and to consider changes in their linguistic practice. These changes are often very inventive: words may be 'reclaimed' either by revaluing their connotations or reviving obsolete definitions, or they may undergo changes in spelling or morphology. Sometimes feminists wage war on a word, while at other times they introduce one. This subversive feminist metalinguistics, a product of the wish to understand and mani pulate language, can be illustrated with a number of specific examples.

INSULTS: VERBAL VIOLENCE AGAINST WOMEN

Many commentators have noted that more words are available to insult women than men; and that generally speaking, taboo words tend to refer to women's bodies rather than men's. Thus for example *cunt* is a more strongly tabooed word than *prick*, and has more tabooed synonyms. Even words like *bugger* and *arsehole* whose reference is male are insulting because they connote homo sexuality, which is not only taboo in itself but associated with femininity as well.

The asymmetry continues. There are terms for women collec tively as sexual prey such as *ass*, *tail*, *crumpet*, *skirt* and *flash*. No such terms exist for men, nor do we have male analogues for *slag*, *tart*, *nympho* or *pricktease*.

Presumably this has something to do with the double standard and the heterosexual state of play in general. Women are thought not to have sexual desires, and if they either show that they do have such desires, or refuse to meet the needs of men, they will be censured. On the other hand they are vilified as prostitutes. Julia Stanley has observed that for English-speakers the prostitute is 'paradigmatic woman'. Male prostitutes have no comparable richness of terminology associated with them, for after all they are far from being paradigmatic men.

To say that the asymmetry of insult terms 'reflects reality', however, would be banal. We need to consider whether general linguistic processes bring it about, and whether its effects on women are significant.

It has been argued by Muriel Schulz that the asymmetry we are considering comes about because of a systematic process of language change called 'semantic derogation'.[5] Terms like *tart* and *harlot* have developed from non-insulting unisex words (*tart*, for instance, was once an endearment like *honey* or *sweetie*). When they became associated with women rather than men, they acquired negative connotations and eventually came to mean *prostitute*.

This process of pejoration can be seen at work in a number of male/female pairs. Whereas the male terms connote power, status, freedom and independence, the female, which in many cases used to be parallel, now cannotes triviality, dependence, negativity and sex.

For instance, *bachelor* (positive, independent, sexual libertine) is opposed to *spinster* (ugly, sexless and frustrated). When the positive aspects of being single came to be associated with women, the term *spinster* seemed so unsuitable that *bachelor girl* had to be coined.

Other examples of semantic non-equivalence are *governor* (powerful, ruler) and *governess* (poor woman looking after children); *master* (competent or powerful man) and *mistress* (sexual and economic dependent); *tramp* (homeless man) and *tramp* (prostitute woman).

The suggestion that politically motivated processes operate systematically in language change is an interesting one for sociolinguists, for it confirms their belief that language change is not a random but a socially significant occurrence which may be discussed in a 'scientific' way. Feminists, however, are likely to find it more interesting that we can reconstruct the history of patriarchy, at least to a small extent, through the history of words.

Yet the feminist analysis of insult terms would be missing something if it stopped there. The existence of so many insulting words for women, many of them meaning the same thing, has a significance over and above what it tells us about cultural beliefs. It is, in fact, itself a form of social control. We can make an analogy here with pornography (since the word *pornography* means 'pictures of prostitutes', perhaps *pornoglossia* would be a good name for the language that reduces all women to men's sexual servants). Feminists have always seen pornography as a symbol of men's desire to objectify and humiliate women. It depicts the woman as an object to be abused, reduces her to body parts and dwells explicitly on rituals of punishment. But more recent analyses of pornographic images (for instance Andrea

Dworkin's *Pornography: Men Possessing Women*)[6] stress that these images *are* violence against women, with effects similar to those of physical violence on women's self-image and attitude. To see degrading images and know men seek them out for pleasure, teaches us that we are despicable, expendable objects. It teaches us that men want to hurt us, and that we had better be afraid.

The same is true of sexual insults. They are verbal violence against women, expressing both our essential qualities in patriarchy (repositories of sexuality, prostitutes) and male woman-hatred, which makes women afraid. Since *cunt* and *slag* are bandied about even more often that the cock and the fist, this violence is no trivial matter, but a source of male power and a means whereby women are daily humiliated.

In several conferences and sessions on language, feminists have discussed this problem and asked how to cope with verbal violence. One solution which has been canvassed for some words is 'reclaiming' – that is, reinvesting a word with a more positive meaning. The word *dyke*, for instance, a disparaging term for Lesbian women, has been rehabilitated to some extent, and there have been suggestions that the same could be done for *cunt*. Women point out its connection with words like *cunning* which carry the idea of power and magic, while others simply say they ascribe positive value to the word *cunt* because it denotes the most female and potent area of their bodies.

Two problems arise with the reclamation approach. First, there is a content problem, for although some words are suitable for celebration, since they refer to revalued conditions of life such as Lesbianism, female anatomy, spinsterhood and so on, many other words are not suitable. Reducing ourselves to body part (e.g. by referring to women as *cunts*) could never be a compliment to our feminist selves. Nor should we glorify the sexual dependence of prostitution.

The second problem is one of *intent*. An important part of the meaning of an insult is the intention behind it, or more precisely what the receiver takes the speaker's intention to have been. We all recognise that what men mean by *cunt* and *dyke* is violent and contemptuous. Just as black people may call themselves *nigger* in friendship (though many, of course, would never do so) without eliminating the racism of the word when white people use it, so we can reclaim certain words amongst ourselves without touching their status as insults in the mouths of men.

LINGUISTIC HERSTORY: RECLAIMING AND REJECTING

It is not only insults that feminists have subjected to close examination and found wanting. Their relationship with many words, and even spellings, demonstrates their consciousness of their meaning and history. Many feminist writers turn frequently to etymological dictionaries to find out when a word entered the language, whether it was coined or borrowed from another language, what it meant and how it has changed.

For instance, in the discussion of the word *cunt* which I mentioned above one woman said that for her, the word and its synonyms conjured up pornographic stories, and therefore she had always used *vagina*. However, she had recently discovered that *vagina* came from Latin, where it meant 'where you sheath your sword'. She found this so offensive that she had abandoned *vagina* as well. And apart from this, she felt she had learned from etymology something about the history of sexism which she did not know before.

In other cases, however, history is deliberately ignored. The word *history* is a good example: feminists often respeak/write it as *herstory*. This reflects the idea that *history* means his-story (so that *herstory* becomes the female equivalent). In fact it comes from Latin *historia* which has no connection with the English word *his*. Similarly, *women* is often spelt by feminists *wimmin*, so that the — *men* element does not appear in it, even though this element is not actually pronounced.

Linguists find this kind of thing irritating (there is no doubt that any attempt to start a 'herstory' course at Harvard would once again cause havoc in the faculty of linguistics) because it is inconsistent – sometimes history is counted as relevant, sometimes not – and in any case they tend to dislike the un-Saussurean view that linguistic history is at all salient for speakers of current English. For feminists, however, the main consideration in using or not using forms like *herstory* ought to be political. *Herstory* is an excellent word in many contexts pointing out with wit and elegance that most history is precisely the story of men's lives; while *wimmin* might be universally applauded as a clever piece of spelling reform, had it not become associated with the unpopular 'extremism' of the women's movement.

The creative use of linguistic structure and linguistic history is a characteristic of much feminist writing. Mary Daly's classic *Gyn/Ecology* is a good example of the 'reclaim and rename' approach: as well as playing on words with great felicity, Daly tries to reclaim obsolete meanings of familiar words like *glamour*, *haggard* and *spinster*. She shows that women's power has been erased from definitions (for instance, the kind of glamour now associated with film stars is a far cry from the magical powers once denoted by the word *glamour*) and wonders why feminists cannot, by the same token, 'wrench back some wordpower' by conscious redefinition.[7] I shall consider this problem (for it is obvious to me that we cannot just redefine in the same way that those with institutional power have done) later in this chapter.

Apart from the 'content and intent' problems we have already touched on, there is a further problem with the work of Daly – many women find it elitist and unreadable. Constant wordplay and extensive terminological definition are not immediately accessible devices, and feminists need to consider very carefully to what extent they are politically productive. (Indeed, as we shall see in later chapters, this is a debate of some importance in current feminism.) Certainly they are not applicable in everyday speech, however well they work in writing.

GAPS IN TERMINOLOGY: SAYING IS BELIEVING

Feminists are hopeful that old words can be given new meanings. But equally, they are hopeful that we can make new words up to name the things that have so far remained unlabelled. For they remind us that if the first principle of sexist language is that female words must be negative, the second is that positive aspects of femaleness should remain unnamed.

In the introduction I referred to the idea of 'naming' to which Adrienne Rich and Dale Spender give so much emphasis. To these writers, it sometimes seems nothing exists until a specific label is hung upon it. I have already said that this strikes me as an extreme claim (and I shall be arguing later that it demonstrates a misunderstanding of the nature of language). Labels may give some sort of social validity to experiences, but the lack of labels does not render any experience ineffable. However, certain terminological lacunae are frequently discussed by feminists because they demonstrate that what naming has been done, has been done from a male viewpoint.

The paradigm example of this sort of discussion concerns terms for sex and sexuality. It is striking, for instance, that what to women is often the most satisfying part of heterosexual love-making is called *foreplay*. For the namer, obviously, this activity comes 'before' the real thing, i.e. penetration, and thus the namer must be a man. Indeed, the word *penetration* betrays male origins; women would have called it *enclosure*! As things stand, most words for the sexual act (itself a revealing term: since when was there only *one* sexual act?) make it into something men do to women: *fuck, poke, screw*. At school I was taught that the word *lover* was not appropriate for women, since it denoted activity, and for the passionate women in Racine's plays we were to use the term *mistress*.

The male slant in the lexicon of sex would be very difficult for anyone to deny, and feminists have made it clear that here, as in other areas, they are dissatisfied. Beyond the sociological analysis of language lies the tantalising possibility of reform: but we must now look at a number of reasons why thorough-going institutional reform of the English lexicon is difficult for any progressive political movement to bring about.

SPREADING THE WORD: THE GATEKEEPERS

A number of processes are common in the history of words. Words are lost: others are invented, either made from old words joined together in new ways (like *palimony* and *denationalise*), borrowed from foreign languages (like *crèche*) or created from the coiner's imagination. The meanings of words (by which I mean the senses listed in dictionaries) do not stay constant for ever, but gradually change. One reason for this is that people do not learn most words from dictionaries but infer their meanings from hearing them used in particular contexts: we may all differ slightly in our beliefs about what words 'really mean'. If enough people infer from reading the word *prevaricate* that it means 'stall, play for time' (to take a recent example discussed in the newspapers), that meaning will challenge the one *prevaricate* is given in dictionaries. It will be no good telling speakers that *prevaricate* 'really means' 'lie' rather than 'stall', because the meaning of words is ultimately a matter of the way the community uses them in talk. Unless they are compulsive users of dictionaries, this will be determined by contextual inference, and meaning will be inherently unstable.

However, it is not true that the process of semantic change operates magically, untouched by anything but the collective mind. Whether new meanings and new words catch on depends to some extent on what means exist to disseminate them. The mass media are powerful in this respect, and so is education (which is currently fighting a rearguard action against the falling together of pairs like *infer/imply* and *disinterested/uninterested*). The dictionary, too, though it cannot be an exhaustive record of what any word 'means', has a certain role to play by legitimating some definitions over others.

The point is that conscious linguistic reform by feminists, or even 'natural' change deriving from women's changing experience and consciousness, is not simply left to take its chance with other social forces affecting language is a free-market competition for semantic supremacy. Any new terms feminists come up with, in order to be institutionalised in the official and public domains of language use, have to pass a number of 'gatekeepers' – the media, education, lexicography – who are very far from being neutral.

The media have sometimes been our allies in spreading new terms and thus new concepts – *sexism*, *sexual harassment*, *battered wives*, *male chauvinism*. They have shown no such enthusiasm for *unwaged*, *double loaded*, *heterosexism*, *male violence* or *patriarchy*, and it is significant that this second set of terms is less widely known than the first outside the women's movement. Moreover, the media have played a large part in pejorating some words that were meant to improve women's position, such as *Ms*, *person* and even *feminist*.

Education is a considerable force in retarding the growth of non-sexist language. Prescriptive rules about generic *he* are enforced as 'grammatical' and many teaching materials still exemplify everything feminists would want to take issue with.

The dictionary is in many ways less influential, since for the majority of English speakers it is an irrelevance. Its sexism, however, is clear. It fails to invest feminist words and definitions with permanence, official sanction and authority, and it contains many negative and offensive definitions of females. Progressives of all stripes should be more aware than they are of the biases that affect the compiling of dictionaries.

It is frequently claimed that dictionaries, like linguistic enterprise in general, are descriptive rather than prescriptive. They merely record the way people use words, without fear or favour. This has sometimes served as an excuse for including very offensive definitions: those who protested at the inclusion of 'Jew' as a verb meaning 'cheat financially' on the grounds that such a definition promoted anti-semitism got short shrift from the disinterested lexicographers in pursuit of English usage. But how accurate is this picture of unbiased scholarship?

The most important bias of dictionaries is toward the written rather than the spoken word. Lexicographers do not begin the quest for current usage in the street or on the bus, but in libraries. Even then they begin their search with literature rather than say, comic books, graffiti or political pamphlets. The consequence is that the coinings of dictionaries are the coinings of those who write literature – middle-class men. The vitality of home and street vernacular is simply ignored. Common words like *skive* and *moonlight* are either absent from dictionaries, or else they are given a special marking as 'colloquial' or 'dialectal'.

The implication here is that the words of educated middle-class speakers are somehow not dialectal (though in fact, if Yorkshire miners speak 'a dialect' so do BBC newsreaders). What dictionaries assume is that while the less privileged will want (need?) to look up the words used by their betters, the reverse is unlikely to be true. No one needs to look up a word it would be beneath her dignity to use. Clearly, then, dictionaries reflect the prejudices of the ruling class.

This is also shown by the definitions they include (and those they do not). Dictionaries in any case foster the illusion that words have a limited number of meanings which can be listed out of context; but worse still, the ones they list tend to be ideologically loaded though they masquerade as objective. For whom, for example, does the word *woman* mean 'weak and lacking in vigour'? Which groups in society concur with the definition of *unfeminine* (as in 'unfeminine hair') as 'not characteristic of women'? What woman considers her clitoris as 'a rudimentary sexual organ in females, analogous to the penis'? (All these definitions came from ordinary dictionaries that are currently on sale, and so probably in current use by schoolchildren, scrabble-players, etc.)

Dictionaries speak only for some people, and their authority is political, not grammatical. This does not mean they are valueless, of course, for arguably those who aspire to educated middle-class usage require a reference book. But they are not the objective and exhaustive record they claim to be. Until we have more control over metalinguistic processes and practices like education and lexicography, we will find it hard to disseminate innovations and changes that we think are desirable, or even see words defined in anything like the way we use them. Feminist reformers, in other words, are put at a disadvantage by the reactionary nature of prescriptive institutions.

GENDER REVISITED: MAKING WOMEN VISIBLE

The best-known aspect of sexism in language is what feminist linguists call 'he/man language': the use of male pronouns as generic or unspecified terms, as in 'no one would do that if he could help it', and the use of *man* and *mankind* to mean the whole human race. A great deal of effort has gone into making institutional changes in this area, since many feminists consider pronouns an important subliminal influence on people's perception of women as secondary or marginal.

Miller and Swift sum up what is wrong with the universal male: 'What standard English usage says about males is that they are the species. What is says about females is that they are a sub-species.'[8] Experiments in linguistics reveal that when faced with generic *man* women consciously exclude themselves from the reference. We equate *man* specifically with males. For many commentators this fact implies that language is more than just trivially offensive: it is able to persuade its speakers that women do not exist. This misleading impression is what reformists set out to correct by means of non-sexist language.

THE MYTH OF NON-SEXIST LANGUAGE

Non-sexist language is language which excludes neither women nor men. It involves recasting words and sentences so that all terminology is neutral. For instance, in a non-sexist formulation *mankind* becomes *humanity*, *craftsman* becomes *artisan*, *spaceman* becomes *astronaut*, *forefathers* become *ancestors* and *chairman* becomes *chairperson* or *chair*. *They* is employed as a singular indefinite pronoun ('no one would do that if they could help it') and generic pronouns are avoided where possible, either by recasting a sentence (e.g. 'pick up baby when he cries' could become 'always pick up a crying baby') or by pluralising ('pick up babies when they cry').

This kind of language is less overtly offensive than the kind it replaces. Nevertheless there are plenty of reasons to suppose that it is ineffective in the sense that it does not really bring women into people's mental landscape at all. The reformists feel that words like *spaceman* have a special place in the lexicon of prejudice. Because *spaceman* incorporates the word *man*, whose meaning has narrowed (become more specialised) from meaning 'person' to meaning 'male person', it strongly suggests a male referent. The implication of *spaceman* is that women cannot fly rockets, walk on the moon, etc. But once the linguistically marked male element *man* is removed, the argument runs, people will not think male any more. The possibility will exist that women can fulfil the new role, non-sexistly designated *astronaut*.

But what if the word *astronaut*, despite having no overt markers of maleness, is used by most people as if it too were male-only? There is a large amount of evidence that this is in fact what happens with words that are not linguistically gender-marked. Consider, for example, the following extracts from newspapers:

The lack of vitality is aggravated by the fact that there are so few able-bodied young adults about. They have all gone off to work or look for work, leaving behind the old, the disabled, the women and the children.

The Sunday Times

A coloured South African who was subjected to racial abuse by his neighbours went berserk with a machete and killed his next-door neighbour's wife, Birmingham Crown Court heard yesterday.

Guardian

In these examples, two phrases without overt linguistic marking of gender are used as if they could only be applied to men: *able-bodied young adult* and *next-door neighbour*. In the first case, the disabled, the old and the non-adult are clearly excluded by the meaning of the words which make up the phrase. But why are women excluded? In the second case, since apparently the murdered woman lived next door to her attacker, why was she not 'the next door neighbour' but just 'the next door neighbour's wife'?

Evidently many language-users, when saying or writing common terms that might in principle refer to either sex, simply do not think of them as referring to women. The words are neutral on the surface, but masculine underneath. Non-sexist language guidelines are a verbal Sex Discrimination Act, in that they legislate on the form of words without being able to alter the meaning. They are a purely cosmetic measure which enables us to see justice being done without really doing us justice.

From where the reformists stand, this must seem very odd. For as we have seen, Miller and Swift *et al.* regard non-sexist language as a necessary and long overdue corrective which will make our speech and writing more accurate: 'The point is not that we SHOULD recognise semantic change, but that in order to be precise, in order to be understood, we must.'[9] Why then should anyone be perverse enough to use words which are not inherently misleading, such as *neighbour* and *adult*, to falsify reality?

Sociologists of literature have pointed out that exactly this question can be asked about popular fiction, for instance the romantic novels bought by large numbers of women.[10] Although most readers would declare these novels realistic in mode, the heroines in fact have attributes not granted to their real-life counterparts. The nurse or secretary in a novel can always maintain a lifestyle superior to anything her real-life salary would allow: she also marries a higher-class, higher-income, more educated man at the end of the book. Is this a deliberate distortion? Is it a sinister plot to misrepresent the world and sustain female false-consciousness?

Feminist discussion on this point stresses the propaganda function of romantic novels, the part they are meant to play in sustaining sexist ideology and their real power to mislead. Hall, however, considers this view naive, simplistic and politically unsophisticated. Hall suggests that literature is not really about faithfully depicting actual states of affairs. Its referent is not the real world so much as the belief-system prevalent in particular parts of it. Far from misrepresenting the world, then, popular literature mirrors the ideological universe of its readers. If this is true of symbolic and representational media generally, it would be entirely beside the point to criticise language for being 'misleading' as to the state of affairs which obtains in the world. Language is not a limpid pool through which the truth may be glimpsed, but a way of representing, a vehicle for 'discourses' and 'ideology'.

Cultures not only tolerate but in many cases seem to demand a contradiction between what people can see for themselves and what they believe to be true, or right. For instance, the notion that women cannot do heavy work (which carries high rates of pay) ought not to cut any ice with women who regularly lift heavy children and stones of shopping, but it does. Women who clean up after incontinent elderly relations ought not to entertain the oft-repeated observation that some jobs are too unpleasant and dirty for women to do, but apparently they accept it. Everyone knows that many women nowadays either choose or are forced to support children on their own: yet women will still say they do not believe in equal pay, because men have families to support. It is not convincing to claim that because women believe incorrect and sexist propositions, they must been misled about the facts.

Miller and Swift believe that language change is threatening because it 'signals widespread changes in social mores'.[11] In fact, few people notice language change, but reform, deliberate intervention for some stated purpose, brings out the Colonel Blimp in many people. This is not necessarily because it 'signals widespread changes in social mores'. Observers in developing cultures report that language lags behind social change, often to the extent that expert 'language planners' are employed.[12] What institutional language reform really signals is an agreement on the part of those who have power to recognise a new 'discourse' or way of understanding things, which challenges the appearance of immutable truth previously enjoyed by the old one.

The outcry which so often attends the demand for linguistic reform comes from those who do not want to be shaken out of the old way of looking at things. If these people are numerous and powerful, strong conservative forces come into play and reform does not succeed.

The cause of such conservatism is only partly anti-feminism, fear of social and political upheaval. Resistance to language change is also related to the way in which people conceptualise language itself as a fixed point in the flux of experience, providing names (their essential correctness guaranteed by history) for phenomena that would otherwise elude our collective grasp. Thus the anthropological linguist Sapir could speak of 'that virtual identity . . . of word and thing which leads to the magic of spells'.[13] And the conservative philosopher Roger Scruton, talking about feminist proposals to reform language, insists, 'Each of us inherits in language the wisdom of many generations. To mutilate this repository of human experience is to mutilate our most fundamental perceptions.'[14]

In the remainder of this book I shall be addressing myself far more to the nature of language itself, and I shall be arguing that this particular view of it is erroneous, an illusion from which people take comfort, but in the end untenable as a theory of language.

POSITIVE LANGUAGE

It should be clear by now that while I feel as excluded as any other woman by 'he/man' language, I cannot put my faith in the non-sexist alternatives which pay only lip-service (literally) to my presence in the world. What sort of changes would I like to make?

The strategy I believe is helpful is the one used in this book – every indefinite or generic referent is feminine. I and several other linguists use this practice all the time. When questioned by people who find it odd, we reply that we are practising positive discrimination through positive language. If it comes naturally to men to say/write *he*, obviously it comes naturally to me to use *she*. In a non-patriarchal world, would we not tend to visualise someone rather like ourselves?

I have no illusions that positive language will change the world. More women will not take up science just because scientists are referred to as *she*. But what might be achieved is a raising of people's consciousness when they are confronted with their own and others' prejudices against saying *she*.

It is still true that women have difficulty in using positive language. (One woman said she could not use it in essays because her subject was theology: on being asked by another woman in the group whether she saw God as male or female, she replied, 'Neither: I see him as an absolute supreme Being!') It seems particularly odd to refer to engineers and astronauts as *she* when everyone knows that the vast majority of them are men; yet when similar untruths are perpetrated by *he* (for instance, when it is used to refer to teachers or hospital patients, most of whom are women) we do not notice.

From time to time, the possibility is mooted of inventing new, sex-indefinite pronouns for the English language (*E*, *tey* and *per* have all been suggested). It is interesting to consider what might happen to such a pronoun in common usage (if indeed it ever caught on).

As we have seen, 'neutral' words tend to make people assume a male referent. So perhaps the new pronoun would be masculinised, and a feminine variant coined. More likely, however, the new pronoun would go the way of the suffix −*person*, whose short history is an object lesson to all reformers. Words like *chairperson* and *sportsperson* were supposed to be sex-neutral replacements for *chairman* and *sportsman*, but in fact they are only ever used for women: Cecil Parkinson is Chairman of the Tory Party, but Joan Ruddock is Chairperson of CND.

It seems that a peculiar odour attaches to the suffix −*woman* even in the humblest of contexts, and −*person* is being used as a sort of euphemism: 'Of course full justice to a steamed pudding can only be done by a true trencherman. The term is used advisedly, for I have never encountered a feminine trencherperson whose curves could easily expand to accommodate a second helping' (*Sunday Times*). In this case, speakers have refused to accept a feminist reform, and indeed have used the letter against the spirit. We are left with a net loss, for if men are spokes*men* while we are spokes*persons*, the presence of women is not being drawn explicitly to anyone's attention. If reclaiming language works, and if it is thought desirable, the word *woman* should be at the top of the list for reclamation.

As many writers have shown, languages and their history are invaluable resources for feminists in their analysis of society. But reform on a wide scale is more problematic, and it is especially unhelpful when it proceeds from simplistic theories about the workings of language in general. As we have seen, supporters of non-sexist' language believe that language exists to represent reality as neutrally/objectively as possible. Therefore, in the interests of accuracy we should strive to include the female half of the human race by replacing male terms with neutral ones. But the 'reality' to which language relates is a sexist one, and in it there are no neutral terms. Words cannot be brought before some linguistic United Nations for definitive judgement; this one is sexist, that is neutral, the other is feminist. Words exist, the theories of linguists notwithstanding, only when they are used. Their meanings are created (within limits, certainly, but pretty elastic limits) by a speaker and hearer in each uniquely defined situation.

For feminists this may prove to be a bitter pill. It means that when we proclaim certain items positive, rehabilitated and so on, we can have no authority outside our own narrow circle, unless the means exist for us to influence the usage of others (and even this is only possible up to a point). In the mouths of sexists, language can always be sexist.

6 Silence, Alienation and Oppression: Feminist Models of Language (I)

> ... thinking is most mysterious, and by far the greatest light we have upon it is thrown by the study of language. This study shows that the form of a person's thoughts are controlled by inexorable laws of pattern of which he is unconscious.
>
> *Benjamin Lee Whorf*

> Without language thought is a vague, uncharted nebula.
>
> *Ferdinand de Saussure*

Sexist language teaches us what those who use it and disseminate it think women's place ought to be: second-class citizens, neither seen nor heard, eternal sex-objects and personifications of evil.

Within the perspective I have labelled 'theoretical reformism', our feminist response is clear. We must expose the 'falseness' of this language, and refuse to tolerate its continued use, providing where necessary a set of neutral, and thus inoffensive, alternatives.

But in Chapter 5 we began to see how this uncomplicated viewpoint failed as a theory of language – as an account of what language does and how it does it. Many feminists now feel a need to go beyond theoretical reformism, developing a more sophisticated analysis of the place of language in culture, and thus in the oppression of women. For these radical theorists there is no neutral language: the entire system, since it belongs to and is controlled by men, is permeated by sexism through and through. Moreover, male language is a species of Orwellian thought-control, for these theorists believe it is through language that we

construct our reality. Those who define the limits of language can
make us see things their way.

It is evident that this more radical view of the nature of
language has become very influential in the women's movement.
A rhetoric of silencing, of appropriation and alienation, pervades
much recent writing. Feminists are convinced that language, or
the lack of an authentic (non-male) language, profoundly affects
women's ability to understand and change their situation.

> The fact is that the female saying 'I' is alien at every moment to
> her own speaking and writing. She is broken by the fact that
> she must enter this language in order to speak or to write. As
> the 'I' is broken, so also is the Inner Eye, the capacity for
> integrity of knowing/sensing. In this way the Inner Voice of the
> Self's integrity is silenced: the external voice babbles in alien
> and alienating tongues.
> . . . Overcoming the silencing of women is an extreme act.[1]

> When we become acutely, disturbingly aware of the language
> we are using and that is using us, we begin to grasp a material
> resource that women have never before collectively attempted
> to repossess. . . . Language is as real, as tangible in our lives as
> streets, pipelines, telephone switchboards, microwaves, radio
> activity, cloning laboratories, nuclear power stations. We
> might hypothetically possess ourselves of every resource on the
> North American continent, but as long as our language is inad
> equate, our vision remains formless, our thinking and feeling
> are still running in the old cycles, our process may be 'revol
> utionary', but not transformative.[2]

In this chapter I want to examine the radical theories upon which
remarks like these are based. Three approaches in particular will
be dealt with: the 'dominant and muted' model of Shirley and
Edwin Ardener; the 'man made language' theory of Dale
Spender; and the psychoanalytic model developed in the wake of
Lacan (which will be discussed in a separate chapter).

While all of these approaches are different, one of the points I
shall be trying to make is that they have a certain amount in
common. They rely, in fact, on three basic principles which are
taken as axiomatic.

First, all three approaches display some degree of linguisti determinism. Language is held to be the primary means by which we make sense of the world, placing significant constraints on our thought and our perceptions. Secondly, it is assumed that men control language, just as they control all other resources in a patriarchal society. It is men who decide what words will mean and who will have the right to use them. That is why language enshrines a male (and misogynist) view of the world.

Thirdly, radical theorists feel that women are put at a disadvantage as speakers and writers. This disadvantage can manifest itself in two ways. On the one hand, women may use the male-controlled language, whose meanings are fixed according to men's experience: if they do, they falsify their own perceptions and experience by putting everything into a male frame of reference. This is alienation. On the other hand, women may try to discuss their experience in an authentically female way. In this case, they soon encounter the lack of a suitable language, and fall silent.

The radical feminist view, then, is of women who live and speak within the confines of a man-made symbolic universe. They must cope with the disjunction between the linguistically-validated male world view and their own experience, which cannot be expressed in male language. Indeed, since language determines reality, women may be alienated not only from language but also from the female experience it fails to encode.

In Chapter 8 I intend to put forward a communicationally oriented alternative theory which does not rely on these axioms of determinism, control and alienation. In this chapter and Chapter 7, however, I want to prepare the ground by explaining radical theories and pointing out their limitations, particularly the questions they leave substantially unanswered. We can begin by looking critically at the background to the crucial problems of linguistic determinism and language control.

DETERMINISM

Linguistic determinism — the idea that language determines perception and thus reality — is an important part of current feminist linguistic theory. However, from the linguist's point of view this raises a number of difficult questions, and needs to be justified rather than assumed. In the section that follows I consider the relation between language and reality, and trace the origins of determinism in linguistic theory.

Language and Reality

The debate on linguistic determinism takes place within the context of a particular view of what reality is. If we believed that reality or the world simply existed 'out there' and that we passively registered it as a series of images with names attached, the question of the effects of language on our perceptions would hardly arise.

In fact, however, modern theories take it for granted that we ourselves play a part in creating 'reality'. Millions of stimuli impinge upon us at every moment: if we were like blank screens, passively receiving every stimulus, our minds would contain an undifferentiated, meaningless chaos. In order to make sense of the world, therefore, we must pay attention selectively, actively choosing, classifying and interpreting incoming stimuli.

The crucial question for the linguist is what part the language a person learns to speak plays in this interpreting/classifying process. To illustrate that this is a real problem, we might consider two opposing possibilities. The first is to see language as a tool we use, a servant of thought. Suppose we use thought (for want of a more precise term) to interpret incoming stimuli, influenced by factors such as the environment, our personal and cultural history, the work we do, etc. Language encodes or expresses this perceived reality. It is simply a medium. In this case there is no great problem about language. It reflects social conditions, and changes in response to social changes.

The second possibility is that language acts like a straitjacket, a ready-made classification which our experience must be forced into, like the Ugly Sister's foot into the deceptively alluring patriarchal glass slipper. The language user engages not with the 'real world', but with a version of it already filtered and, given that powerful groups control it, distorted, by the language. In this case language is a problem. It effectively creates our perceptions of reality, and they can produce a repressive and one-sided picture.

Feminists and many other progressives have for some time

tended towards the second possibility rather than the first. Their theories derive from the work of earlier writers, especially Lacan (and thus Saussure), Whorf and Sapir. We must now turn to those theories and ask two questions about them: first, what they say and what arguments exist for and against them; and second, how far the feminists who have taken them up remain faithful to their original meaning and spirit.

The roots of determinism: Saussure and Lacan

Saussure is often claimed as the founder-member of the determinist camp. Certainly he rejected in the *Cours* the simplistic first alternative, that language simply gives form to ideas:

> Psychologically, our thought – apart from its expression in words – is only a shapeless and indistinct mass. Philosophers and linguists have always agreed in recognising that without the help of signs we would not be able to make a clear-cut, consistent distinction between two ideas. Without language thought is a vague, uncharted nebula. There are no pre-existing ideas, and nothing is distinct before the appearance of language. The characteristic role of language with respect to thought is not to create a material phonic means for expressing ideas, but to serve as a link between thought and sound.[3]

But how far Saussure can really be called determinist is open to question. Even if he is correct in asserting that thought without language is formless and vague (can aphasics, deaf-mutes and animals with problem-solving abilities 'think' and is their 'thought' an uncharted nebula?) and that there are no innate or pre-existing ideas, he seems to be saying not that language determines thought but that the two are inseparable.

For neo-Saussureans like Lacan, the determinism of Saussure lies in his doctrine that the sign is arbitrary, functioning only in a system of signification. The whole continuum of experience is segmented in an arbitrary way by the signifiers of the language; and since for Lacan our entry into the world of experience is effected by learning a language, that arbitrary classification is the one that becomes our reality. As Marks and de Courtivron observe, for the Lacanian 'meaning is located not in the thoughts of the enunciator but in the system of signs itself'.[4] The world into which we are socialised is not a world of the things themselves, but a symbolic order fixed by the linguistic system.

This need not be accepted without question. Learning language could be a matter of imposing one (linguistic) symbolic order on a prior order with different, or multiple, determinants. One linguist, Ian Griffiths, speaks of language exploiting a 'jigsaw principle' (i.e. words are cut *across* the pattern one would naturally use to make sense of reality, just as one tries to cut a picture in non-obvious ways when one is making a jigsaw puzzle). He observes,

> The fundamental Saussurean misbegotten structural semantic fallacy is that words represent an amorphous undifferentiated reality ... the jigsaw principle on the contrary requires an intrinsically highly structured pre-patterned reality across which the lexical order can cut.[5]

Saussure certainly did locate meaning outside any one individual language user. *Langue* for him was a collective phenomenon, 'the social side of speech, outside the individual who can never create nor modify it by himself'.[6] However, it is unclear whether he would have subscribed to all the implications of this manoeuvre. We must return later to the rigid separation of meaning and the individual from which so much Lacanian theory springs.

The roots of determinism: Sapir and Whorf

Within linguistics, the doctrine of determinism is associated not with Saussure but with the American anthropological linguists Sapir and Whorf. Indeed, the idea itself is often labelled 'Whorfian' and known technically as the 'Sapir–Whorf hypothesis'.

Sapir–Whorfian determinism reflects a rather different set of preoccupations from those of Saussure and the semiologists. Its starting point is not the linguistic postulate that each language is a system of differences but the empirical observation of various cultures. The question for Sapir and Whorf, both of whom studied native American culture extensively, was why the populations they observed seemed to have such different perceptions of 'the same' realities. Their answer was that linguistic differences determined differences in world view.

> Human beings are very much at the mercy of the particular language which has become the medium of expression for their society.... The fact of the matter is that the 'real world' is to a large extent unconsciously built up on the language habits of the group. No two languages are ever sufficiently similar to be considered as representing the same social reality. The worlds in which different societies live are different worlds, not the same world with different labels attached.[7]

It is significant that Sapir uses the word 'unconsciously': he implies that to reconceptualise the world outside your own particular language is difficult because speakers have no awareness of the kinds of distortion language causes. Whorf, too, stresses the unfreedom of the individual: 'no individual is free to describe nature with absolute impartiality but is constrained to certain modes of interpretation even when he thinks himself most free'.[8] Yet Sapir did not feel, as later feminist enthusiasts of determinism appear to do, that what is unconscious must remain always hidden and unchallenged. He implied that it was the mark of an advanced culture that it could generate forms of knowledge that transcend the tyranny of grammar: 'as our scientific experience grows we must learn to fight the implications of language'.[9]

Sapir–Whorfian determinism is rather different from the Saussurean brand. For the Saussurean, language is an autonomous system which replaces the world of things, an intermediary between brute reality and human perception. The more anthropologically inclined Whorfian, however, sees language as a mode of action that interpenetrates with experience to the extent that words *are* things.

Whorfian determinism also stresses different things from those which interest the Saussurean. For instance, Whorf is much more concerned with patterns of sentence structure, the subtle distinctions expressed by grammatical particles, etc., than with the meaning of individual signs or words.[10] For Whorf the implications of grammar escape the language user much more easily than those of lexical meaning (and to this the post-

Chomskyan linguist would add that syntactic patterns are learned in a much more rigid and less idiosyncratic way). For Saussure, however, they would have been a matter of *parole* and thus not determining in the same way.

It might well be asked what evidence Sapir and Whorf put forward for their particular deterministic views. As I have already observed, their work was mainly on American Indian communities, and the most famous Whorfian study is Whorf's own study of the Hopi.

Whorf focused on a number of things about the Hopi, particularly their very un-European conception of time (they did not see that one could have a quantity of time, or cut the time dimension into segments). Whorf explained this peculiarity with reference to the Hopi language, which has no tense system.

The most obvious question this raises is whether Whorf did not put his linguistic cart before his conceptual horse. In other words, perhaps the Hopi, for historical and economic reasons, developed a way of life in which the European concept of time was an irrelevance; and therefore grammatical tense never entered their language.

This point can be made even more clearly with reference to the well-known observation that Eskimos (Inuit) have a multiplicity of terms for snow. Although having a vast number of terms for something may help you to perceive its gradations in an ordered way, clearly the terms must have been invented in the first place because they were useful and necessary in the circumstances of Inuit life. Discussion of this point is not just nitpicking. A Whorfian outlook is useful as a corrective to the common-sense view of language as a transparent medium for expressing thoughts and perceptions; but it is important to define the limits of determinism.

Two questions in particular seem pertinent. First, if signifiers do cut up the conceptual universe differently in different languages, is this completely arbitrary or does it reflect facts about a culture which are obviously non-linguistic? (the Inuit are a good example here: for it would surely be very remarkable if instead of having a lot of words for snow they had a selection of terms for horse-hide). Second, how great is our ability to see around the categorisation scheme of our language? It is relatively easy or relatively hard to make interpretations that are at odds with your language?

These questions are relevant to the feminist debate on whether language reflects or causes women's oppression. If language segments the conceptual universe in accordance with non-linguistic cultural norms (e.g. sexual differentiation of an extreme kind, and the devaluing of women) then it is not inculcating a world view but obeying the dictates of one. And if it is not difficult to reject the cultural assumptions built into your language then even its power to reinforce those norms must be limited, and we must look for non-linguistic reasons why they persist.

A number of arguments have been marshalled against the Sapir–Whorf hypothesis. One is a belief in universals of language: if you believe that languages are at bottom all very similar, because all speakers have the same mental apparatus, it would be awkward to have to admit that the undeniably diverse perceptions of different communities were determined by their languages. Universals have been an article of linguistic faith ever since Chomsky, and serious engagement with Whorfian ideas has consequently ground to a halt.

The second argument, whose proponents do not necessarily have to believe in linguistic universals, concerns translation and language learning. Once again, no one denies that there will be a certain amount of cultural relativity. Since speakers of different languages do undoubtedly inhabit differing worlds to some extent, they will certainly have diverse ways of interpreting reality which complicate the process of translation from one language to another. Lyons representatively observes that 'true bilingualism implies the assimilation of two cultures'.[11]

If one adopted an absolute determinism, however, translation and second-language learning would have to be made out more difficult than is actually the case. Consider, for example, the case of a Hopi learning English. Until she understands our conception of time she will not be able to use the tense system correctly: but in a totally Whorfian world she cannot understand our conception of time without mastering the English tense system! If we are not to be caught in this kind of paradox we must set some limits to our belief in determinism.

Finally, there is an argument from the creativity of language users, which leads to language change. It is clear that as conditions alter, speakers can and do modify both their frame of reference and their language. Nor do they do this simply by adding new elements to the existing stock: often the meanings of old elements shift. Remoulding of our linguistic classification system is constantly being undertaken. Perhaps, then, determinists err in believing, as George Orwell put it, 'that language is a natural growth and not an instrument which we shape for our own purposes'.[12]

CONTROL

If the first assumption of feminist theories of language is determinism, the second is control. Radicals believe that the deterministic powers of language may be exploited, and routinely are exploited, by the privileged groups who control language for political ends. This proposition of control would be more precisely expressed as two claims. The first is that powerful groups can appropriate language in the same way they can appropriate, say, financial resources; while the second is that by doing so they are able to exercise subliminal control over their subordinates and maintain their own power. Both these claims will be fully discussed within the critique presented in Chapter 8: what is of interest at this point, however, is the nature and status in our culture of the idea that language functions essentially as a means of political control.

Within linguistics there has never been a debate on control comparable with the debate on determinism (perhaps because determinism has been rather unpopular, and control is seen to depend on it to a great extent). It might then seem all the more remarkable that feminist theories take control, or more precisely male control, for granted. In fact, of course, the idea of control is too entrenched in liberal humanist thought to need any validation from linguistic science. It has passed into the realms of accepted wisdom.

The 'control through language' argument is normally deployed in the ongoing debate about democracy and totalitarianism. Commentators equate totalitarianism with a language under strict control (some even go so far as to suppose that a 'corrupt' language gives rise to totalitarianism); conversely, the defence of language constantly undertaken by writers, critics, philosophers and journalists is put forward as a defence of democratic values. For the liberal humanist, a totalitarian state is not just one where you may not say what you like (e.g. because you will be put in prison and forced to recant) but more terrifyingly, one where you literally cannot say what you like, because the state or other repressive agency has control of the words you would say it in.

A good example of this type of argument is to be found in a *Times* article by the philosopher and Tory pundit Roger Scruton, titled (with an obligatory bow to Orwell, the major populariser of the whole idea during this century) 'How Newspeak leaves us naked'.[13] The article purports to review a Soviet dictionary, the Novosti Press Agency's *Short Guide to Political Terms*, and thus it is basically an attack on state control of the language: since Scruton is a Conservative, however, it also attributes linguistic 'imperialism' to English political groupings, especially the women's movement.

Scruton opens by demonstrating that he believes in determinism, and in conscious conspiracies to subvert language by left-wing extremists: 'If you want to control the world, first control language: such has been the unspoken maxim of revolutionary politics in our century.' His major aim is to show that there has been such a conspiracy of Soviet lexicographers to undermine the 'true' meanings of words like *democracy* and *liberalism*, so that anything other than Party dogma becomes literally unspeakable:

> Its purpose is to forestall refutation by securing an unshakeable bridgehead in language. Communism ... has tried to ensure that the words of politics can be used only to express dogmas of its own- not because it believes those dogmas to be true, but because it wants lies to take the place of truth.

Scruton typically takes it for granted that there *is* an unshakeable bridgehead in language. Once you have corrupted the system, you have taken away all your adversaries' resources: 'all rival creeds are to be appropriated and devoured; no words will express them, since no words will be available that have not been enslaved by falsehood.'

Although presumably radical theorists would violently disagree with Scruton's views on the Novosti *Guide*, they would be on remarkably shaky theoretical ground in doing so. For after all, what is the difference between the apocalyptic view expressed by Scruton and the feminist belief that men have appropriated the language? The progressive and the reactionary are locked into the same view of their object.

Another preoccupation the reactionary shares with the progressive is with the supreme value and importance of language. Scruton observes, 'one is struck by the outrage that communism has committed against language'. Feminists similarly feel that language is extraordinarily powerful and important: 'how can we conceive of a revolutionary struggle that does not involve a revolution in discourse?'[14] Language is not unimportant, but nevertheless there is something very distasteful about such language-olatry. Outrages cannot be committed against languages but only against their speakers. Marks and de Courtivron, comparing the French and American traditions, observe that few English-speaking feminists 'can believe in the reduction of reality – oppression, suffering – to language'.[15] It is important to consider, as linguistically-based radical feminism becomes more popular, whether this common-sense American attitude does not have a good deal to recommend it.

Just as a feminist theory of language must engage very seriously with the problem of linguistic determinism, confronting and dealing with the difficult questions it raises, so it must engage with the notion of control. As I have been trying to show, the idea that language, or more specifically meaning, can be manipulated to obliterate dissent is very ingrained, so much so that to imagine an alternative model of language and its relation to politics is almost impossible. Nevertheless, feminists must ask a number of questions about the accepted model. How do men effect control of languages and how does it work in practice? Are there limits to it? How important is it relative to other forms of control? Finally, what view of language does it presuppose to talk about male control, and is this view tenable?

Determinism and control are the twin foundation stones on which feminist theories of women's oppression, alienation and silence are built. It is time now to look at some of those theories, paying attention to the forms of determinism and control they postulate, and not forgetting the general background problems we have been discussing.

DOMINANT AND MUTED: WOMEN'S REALITY, MEN'S REPRESENTATION

The 'dominant and muted' model proposed by anthropologist

Shirley and Edwin Ardener has been very influential; although it is not itself the product of radical feminism, it is cited by such radical theorists as Dale Spender and Cheris Kramarae in their own analyses. The basic premise of the dominant/muted model is that while every group in a society generates its own ideas about reality at a deep level, not all of these can find expression at a surface level because the 'mode of specification' or communicative channel is under the control of the dominant group. In the case of men and women, women are in this relatively less articulate position: they are, in the words of the Ardeners, a 'muted group' whose reality does not get represented.

> This dominant model may impede the free expression of alternative models of the world which subdominant groups may possess, and perhaps may inhibit the very generation of such models. Groups dominated in this sense find it necessary to structure their world through the model (or models) of the dominant group, transforming their own models as best they can in terms of the received ones.[16]

So briefly, the Ardeners believe that women do generate a reality of their own, but have no means of encoding it linguistically. They have to perform a sort of translation into the male mode of specification.

The Ardeners have been at pains to point out that linguistic *silence* is not the defining characteristic of a muted group: 'They may speak a great deal. The important issue is whether they are able to say all they would wish to say, where and when they wish to say it.'[17] The point is that for whatever reason, muted groups such as women do not generate a mode of specification, and their expression of their experience is structured by someone else's language: 'the muted structures are "there", but cannot be "realised" in the language of the dominant structure.'[18] Three questions seem to me to arise from this account of what Shirley Ardener has called 'differing orders of perception'. For the anthropologist they may be of marginal interest only, but for the linguist, or the feminist, they are vital.

The problem of determinism

It is clear that the dominant/muted model is not radically

deterministic, for after all it is axiomatic that 'the muted
structures are there', and this would seem to rule out any notion
that language determines thought or perception. It is interesting
to note, though, the degree of equivocality the Ardeners display
on this question, particularly in Shirley Ardener's later paper
'The nature of women in society'. Here she observes, 'Words
which continually fall on deaf ears may, of course, in the end
become unspoken, or even unthought.'[19] The hint of determinism
is even stronger a page later when Ardener enquires, 'Are they
[women] able to think in ways which they would have thought
had they been responsible for generating the linguistic tools with
which to shape their thoughts?'[20]

There is a vagueness here, or maybe even a contradiction. For
if we are to think of language as shaping people's thoughts, given
that there is no language to encode what women think, why
should the muted structures be 'there' at all? Should not male
domination of language ensure that everyone's model be the
same? And if on the other hand language does not determine
people's thoughts (so that alternative models would be predicted
by the theory) we are left with the rather perplexing question of
why women, and other muted groups, *can* generate underlying
models of reality but *cannot* generate a mode of specification to
express them.

The problem of control

It is this problem which seems to me at once the most important
and the most intractable within the Ardener model. It simply
not clear that a linguistic reason exists why women who are able
to generate a model of reality independent of the male model
cannot also generate independent ways of representing their
reality linguistically. Indeed, it is not even clear that women do
not in fact generate languages with which to represent both their
reality and their separate female identity. The paper in which
Edwin Ardener initiates the whole discussion actually deals with
such a language, the secret Liengu (mermaid) language of
Bakweri women.[21] Other examples exist, and the sex differences
now coming to light may also reflect women's conscious efforts to
tailor language to their own models.

The implications of remarks made by both the Ardeners is that women's inarticulacy results from men's control over language. However, it is also possible to find an alternative suggestion to the effect that men do not control meaning at all. Rather, women *elect* to use modes of expression men can understand, because that is the best way of getting men to listen.

> . . . there are dominant modes of expression in any society which have been generated by the dominant structures within it. In any situation, only the dominant mode of the relevant group will be 'heard' or 'listened to'. The 'muted groups' in any context, if they wish to communicate, must express themselves in terms of this mode, rather than in ones which they might otherwise have generated independently.[22]

So in this case we are discussing a social rather than an individual or mental suppression of female language: it is not that women are unable to encode their experience, but that to do so is socially unproductive and politically inexpedient.

The linguistic data on all sorts of muted groups tend to suggest that they *do* generate specific modes of language use, but engage in 'code switching' in order to function in societies where they are subordinated. Women together can talk about their experience and may even share (like the Bakweri mermaid women) ritual channels of communication which men cannot understand or may not use. Women with men, however, will indeed practise translation, for as Shirley Ardener says, 'Unless their views are presented in a form acceptable to men . . . they will not be given a proper hearing.'[23] No one could possibly claim, of course, that this was not itself an important disadvantage. It is obvious, for instance (and the Ardeners point it out more than once), that having to translate from one code into another handicaps women in the public domain where linguistic exchanges are regulated by conventions and traditions of an essentially man-made nature. However, it is important to grasp the difference between saying on the one hand, that women lack the means to express their world view in language and are thus muted in society, and saying on the other hand that women are muted because the kind of language they use is unacceptable to men. To make the first assertion is to claim that women have a linguistic problem; to make the second assertion is to say that the problem is not one of language but one of power.

The problem of power

The question of power is the one the Ardeners appear to shy away from. They seem reluctant to consider that dominant groups are dominant for some reason. Shirley Ardener observes, '...the present way of distinguishing a dominant from a muted... model does not impose upon us an obligation to talk in terms of "domination by men" or "the oppression of women" where this is taken to be a purposeful male activity'.[24] This reluctance to face the facts which are detailed in her own work is less trivial than it might appear.[25] Talk of 'structures of dominance' rather than 'the oppression of women' is consistent with the idea that muting is a technical and linguistic phenomenon caused by structural factors in a society, namely the ability of dominant groups to retain control of language. If alternatively we were to regard muting as a partial and situationally determined constraint placed by women on their own self-expression as a survival tactic because men reject *their* communicative channel, we would expect to see some kind of coercion, some means of inculcating female constraint and negative value judgements on women's talk, available to dominant groups by virtue of their general position of power. The social rules and taboos used in many cultures to silence women (see Ardener[25] and Zimmerman and West[26]) fit this description exactly, and it is a pity that the dominant/muted model does not go into the implications of these practices more thoroughly.

LINGUISTIC DEVELOPMENTS: CHERIS KRAMARAE

In her book *Women and Men Speaking*, the linguist Cheris Kramarae attempts to formulate linguistic hypotheses based on the dominant/muted model, and to examine the evidence for each. The hypotheses she thinks follow from the Ardeners' theory are these:

1   Women have difficulty in public speaking (because male language is mandatory).
2   Men have more difficulty understanding what women mean than vice versa (because members of muted groups have to be

aware of dominant *and* muted models, whereas the reverse is not true).

3   Women express dissatisfaction with dominant modes of expression and search for alternatives.[27]

Kramarae concludes that women are not less fluent than men in public speaking (a rather strange conclusion, one would have thought) but that perhaps this is because they have developed superior skills to compensate for the need to translate from female to male models. On the other two hypotheses she is more definite, feeling that there is evidence to support both. She points out that in anecdote, sociological survey and clinical practice alike, men continually express their inability to discover what women think or want. Women express no such misgivings about men.

But what kind of support does this give to a specifically linguistic theory? Given that most women depend for their material and emotional support on intimate knowledge of what men want, it seems an unsurprising observation. Kramarae certainly produces little evidence that it has anything to do with the ways in which the sexes express themselves linguistically.

On the last hypothesis, that women are dissatisfied with dominant modes of communication and are searching for alternatives, Kramarae relies heavily on the attitudes of present-day women's groups. As she points out, feminists have usually done away with formal speaking arrangements and the rhetoric of traditional male-dominated politics. Women writers, too, have made particular genres their own (especially the novel and the diary).

The dominant/muted model of the Ardeners has a lot to offer feminists, but it also contains much that is vague and misleading. The Ardeners clearly show that man-made rules and institutions limit the settings and situations in which women may effectively speak, and they suggest that muted groups are obliged either to translate into dominant modes of speech or be ignored. They avoid the most problematic excesses of linguistic determinism and place a realistic emphasis on the point many theorists overlook, that women do actually have a model of reality and, far from being passive and silent victims of muting, they may in fact develop ritual channels for dealing with their experience.

What the model really fails to show is that muted groups lack a language, and that dominant groups are able to appropriate all linguistic resources. The alternative suggestion, that women communicate adequately with each other but are institutionally constrained/negatively judged in the public (male) arena, is much more plausible.

MAN MADE LANGUAGE: PATRIARCHY AND THE POWER OF DEFINITION

Dale Spender, whose book *Man Made Language* must be the best-known text on women and language, is at once more radical and more forthright than the Ardeners. Whereas the Ardeners' notions of determinism and control are largely implicit, often vague and unexplained, Dale Spender is not afraid to spell out her belief in determinism and her ideas on how men control language. The Man Made Language theory exemplifies all the three points I mentioned earlier. According to Dale Spender, it is through their control over meaning that men are able to impose on everyone their own view of the world; women, without the ability to symbolise their experience in the male language, either internalise male reality (alienation) or find themselves unable to speak at all (silence).

Determinism

Determinism is not so much argued as assumed, though the usual case for it is set out at length:

> Language is our means of classifying and ordering the world: our means of manipulating reality. In its structure and in its use we bring our world into realisation, and if it is inherently inaccurate, then we are misled. If the rules which underlie our language system, our symbolic order, are invalid, then we are daily deceived.
> Yet the rules for meaning, which are part of language, are not natural; they were not present in the world and merely awaiting discovery by human beings. On the contrary, they had to be invented before anything could be discovered, for without them there is no frame of reference, no order, no possibility for systematic interpretation and understanding.[28]

But although initially the rules had to be invented, it is clear that for Spender they are not invented afresh by each generation of language users. They exist as a fixed system which is learnt by children in the course of their socialisation: '. . . these rules have a habit of becoming self-validating and self-perpetuating, regardless of any misapprehensions on which they may have been based.'[29]

In Spender's symbolic order one does not construct meaning, one 'enters' it: and since it embodies the male world view, having originally been made by men, we unconsciously build up ways of seeing and thinking which fit in with such a view:

> While at one level we may support or refute the myth of male superiority – it being a matter of political choice – at another level we are unaware of the way in which it structures our behaviour and forms some of the limits of our world. With the crucial underlying rule that the world can be divided into plus male and minus male categories we have seen the construction of patriarchal order. It is a symbolic order into which we are born, and as we become members of society and begin to enter the meanings which the symbols represent, we also begin to structure the world so that those symbols are seen to be applicable: we enter into the meaning of patriarchal order and we then help to give it substance, we help it to come true.[30]

It is noticeable that Spender draws on a number of different strands of determinism. The concept of a symbolic order which we enter is Lacanian; but elsewhere Spender insists on her debt to Sapir and Whorf.

> On the one hand there is the evidence that not all human beings are led to the same view of the world by the same physical evidence and on the other hand is the explanation – namely the Sapir–Whorf hypothesis – that this is because of language. It is language which determines the limits of our world, which constructs our reality.[31]

Yet she is much more extreme than Sapir, apparently believing that the constraints imposed by language cannot be escaped:

> Human beings cannot impartially describe the universe because in order to describe it they must first have a

classification system. But paradoxically, once they have that classification system, once they have a language, THEY CAN SEE ONLY CERTAIN ARBITRARY THINGS.[32]

This very strong determinism is the background to all Dale Spender's ideas about language.

Control

Spender's central claim, however, is that men control language and in particular, meaning. Women have been systematically excluded from the making of meanings. This is explained with reference to a particular view of how knowledge is constructed, put forward by Dorothy Smith:

> This is how a tradition is formed. A way of thinking develops in this discourse through the medium of the printed word as well as in speech. It has questions, solutions, themes, styles, standards, ways of looking at the world. These are formed as the circle of those present builds on the work of the past. From these circles women have been excluded...deprived of the means to participate in creating forms of thought relevant or adequate to express their own experience or to define ... their situation and concerns. They have never controlled the material or social means to the making of a tradition among themselves or to acting as equals in the ongoing discourse of intellectuals.[33]

It is alleged that men build up a tradition of received wisdom – facts, theories, ways of seeing and interpreting – by checking their contributions with other men. No one in the charmed circle is likely to ask himself, or anyone else, what women think and whether pieces of knowledge concerned with women strike the female population as fair and accurate.

As an account of female non-participation in academic/ intellectual life, this is fair enough. One glance around any university, one look at any intellectual TV or radio broadcast will reveal that charmed circles contain precious few women. It is also impossible to forget that until recently men were able to deny us, by statute, entry to the professions, to higher education, before that to any education, even simple literacy. It is true that the material means (money, educational resources) and the social means (freedom from male persecution and ridicule) never have existed for women to participate in academic life on an equal footing with men: indeed they still do not exist.

It is surely not true, though, that women have never had a tradition of their own. Of the thousands burned as witches, for instance, many were punished precisely because they possessed traditional knowledge which was denied to men. But in any case, what is at issue is not Smith's highly institutionalised 'knowledge', which can indeed be regulated by legal provisions and financial considerations, but *language*. It is not at all clear that Smith's analysis of the construction of meanings within the intellectual tradition will do as a model of how the meanings of language are constructed in everyday interaction. Everyday language is not the same thing as the ongoing discourse of intellectuals, and Spender needs to explain how the same processes of exclusion and validation can go on in both. This is a matter I shall return to in the next chapter. Nevertheless, the man-made language theory states that men and men alone define meanings from their vantage point of difference and dominance. For women, these meanings are false and alienating, as Spender tries to show by considering the word *motherhood*.

According to Spender, men have built a 'positive' meaning into the word *motherhood* which makes it impossible for women to discuss, or even mentally acknowledge, any negative experiences they might have of being mothers. The male-ordained meaning of the word ensures that 'unhappy motherhood' is a contradiction in terms. The clash between what a woman knows of motherhood and what she knows the word means forces her into silence. Her own meaning is outside the norms of language; might her experience be abnormal also? If she speaks the truth, will she be labelled as unnatural and deviant as the phrase 'unhappy motherhood?'

Dale Spender believes that the entire lexicon can be analysed like this: every single meaning is literally man-made, and, inevitably then, words encode a male point of view which is often at odds with female experience. This is the source of alienation and silence; in a man-made language you either see things through male eyes or you reject existing words, silencing yourself. Spender believes that men encode in language not only their world view but their conviction they are superior to women. This is achieved by an all-embracing semantic rule that anything to do with women becomes negatively marked and pejorated. Women and men thus learn to perceive the world through a haze not just of maleness but of misogyny.

The great unanswered questions in this model of meaning are: how is meaning made, and how is meaning learned? It surely cannot he a matter of men writing dictionaries and women looking up words in them, since that is not how anyone learns to speak. But if men can infer meaning directly from their own experience, the theory denies women that possibility. If women constructed meanings according to their experience they would have ideas about words very different from men's, and it is crucial to this theory that in fact they should learn the alien male definitions, which force them to internalise a male world view. How then do they do it?

Spender would presumably fall back here on the neo-Saussurean notion of 'entering' meanings which are already available to your society as a fixed symbolic order, rather as you might learn the traditional folktales of your culture. Yet this just pushes the problem back in time: how was the symbolic order constructed and by whom? Ultimately Spender's answer must be 'by men' and some account of this must be given.

Power

The mystery of why women have not encoded meanings based on their own experience deepens when we consider Spender's apparent belief that they can and should start to do so immediately as a political strategy. The blurb of *Man Made Language* enthuses, 'once women expose the falseness of male meanings and encode their own, language and society can assume new forms, and women can move towards autonomy and self determination'. In Spender's work it is always rather unclear whether women are without linguistic resources because they are without power (in which case they cannot change language without changing their status first) or whether they need linguistic resources before they can increase their power. Although Spender gives considerable weight to the Whorfian notion that a patriarchal reality is constructed primarily through a patriarchal language, sometimes she hints that linguistic systems are purely superstructural:

'Any exposure of the false nature of male superiority, while not a direct attack on male power, is an indirect attack which undermines it. If and when sufficient members of society no longer act in a manner which acquiesces in that superiority and permits it to go unchallenged. . . that power will need to be defended or transformed.'[34]

In this formulation Spender reminds us that male superiority is not male power, but the justification of it. Language is a means of upholding not power but the notion of superiority that makes power look natural or fair. Undermine language and you force men to defend their power in some other way, or to change its nature; you expose the myth of superiority for what it is, thus inciting women to attack male power, now revealed as *non*-natural and *un*fair.

This is a far cry from Rich or Cixous, who consider women's 'meanings' transforming in themselves. It is a shrewd account of why we should dismantle cultural prejudices as well as sexist institutions. So it is hard to see why Dale Spender lands herself with the apparatus of linguistic determinism, which does indeed confuse the power with the myth that justifies it.

These Whorfian/radical feminist versions of determinism, male control and female alienation belong, both intellectually and politically, to the Anglo-American tradition. In the next chapter we must consider a rather different framework, where problems of femininity and male power are located in relation to a radical concept of what language is, and what part it plays in human affairs.

7 Feminist Models of Language (II): Semiology and the Gendered Subject

> One is born in a language and
> the language speaks us, dictates
> to us its law...
>
> *Hélène Cixous*

> All Western discourse presents
> a certain isomorphism with the
> masculine sex.
>
> *Luce Irigaray*

In recent years there has been much more widespread awareness than ever before of a serious challenge to the linguistic and anthropological tradition of Shirley Ardener, Dale Spender and their colleagues throughout the English-speaking world. That challenge comes from the discipline I have been calling 'semiology', and what it claims to offer through a synthesis of Freud, Marx and Saussure, is an explanation of the human subject him- or her-self.

Trying to explain semiology to a non-specialist audience, especially in relation to mainstream positivist linguistics, is a project fraught with difficulties, not just because semiology is complex and sophisticated with its own extensive terminology, but also because the shift of viewpoint necessitated by any such explanation may well do the less immediately graspable paradigm a covert injustice. As Coward and Ellis, themselves the authors of an introductory text, observe,

> The flood of translations and of introductions in layman's terms (i.e. within another conceptual framework, according to

another view of the world) is witness to more than just a desire
to neutralise this work. It shows that the traditional disciplines
. . . are dissatisfied with their own methodology and want to
import a controlled dose of new concepts that can cope with
'problems' that have arisen. These traditional disciplines
appropriate concepts in a piecemeal fashion to paper over their
cracks, when in reality the cracks bear witness to the weakness
of their theoretical foundations. . . . The result is . . . traditional
British eclecticism.[1]

It must be all or nothing, Coward and Ellis imply. The reader
must try to enter into the semiologist's universe, and cannot expect to judge what she finds there by the same standards she has
used outside. Simplification will always be over-simplification,
and explanation 'in layman's terms' risks being called reductive
by those more familiar with the framework.

Nevertheless, it is essential to give some account of semiological
theory. Its recent concern with the construction of sexual identity
in the developing subject, and its insistence on a linguistic basis
for that process of construction, makes it extraordinarily relevant,
a theory that speaks to feminist concerns. And indeed, it has been
appropriated by several feminist tendencies. No discussion of
feminism and linguistic theory would now be complete if it did
not pay close attention to these developments.

As a relatively easy way into the sophistication of theories based
on Marx and Freud as well as Saussure, we may consider some of
the specific disagreements between semiologically oriented writers
and Anglo-American sociolinguistics. These emerge rather clearly
from a review article on Dale Spender's *Man Made Language* that
appeared in *Screen Education* under the authorship of Maria
Black and Rosalind Coward.[2] In taking exception to Spender's
account of language and women's oppression, Black and Coward
reveal preoccupations typical of the semiological approach. They
object particularly to Spender's 'simplistic' notion of *power*, and
to her empirical and mechanistic interpretation of *meaning*.

POWER

The dispute about power, is not, perhaps, strictly linguistic, but it does emphasise the important fact that Anglo-American and French writers typically embrace very different concepts of feminism. Dale Spender's is what might be termed 'radical feminism': it posits a social organisation in which all men have power over all women, deriving from their right to exploit women materially in marriage, and from the use, actual or threatened, of institutionally sanctioned physical violence.[3] Black and Coward's feminism owes more to later marxist models (and particularly to the ideas of Louis Althusser and Michel Foucault) in which social organisation is a complex matter structured by ideologies – sets of representational practices which construct power relations without needing to resort to obvious coercion. Although the sexual power relation is constructed to men's advantage, theorists in the Black and Coward mould would think it vulgar to implicate all men in its construction, or even in the exercise of power over all women. They would stress the extent to which we are all constructed, and the many different dimensions of power simultaneously operative in one society. It is in this context that we can understand Black and Coward's objection to Spender assuming 'that one group literally has power over the other'.[4]

MEANING

Both Dale Spender and the Ardeners contend that women generate (or would generate) different meanings because their experiences of the world are different. The problem is that men control the processes by which meanings are encoded in language, and therefore language represents only male experience, excluding female 'meanings'.

For Black and Coward, it is simply incoherent to talk about meaning in this way, as if it simply arose from experience, innocent of language or of ideology. Meanings for them are made possible by language, and language structures, rather than expressing, the individual's experience:

[Dale Spender's] understanding of language is problematic assuming as it does that 'meanings' derive from clear-cut groups, generated by their different social experiences. . . Meanings reflect the individual's experience of reality and are simply expressed in language. The communality of meanings ...is seen as an effect of groupings of individuals with structurally similar experiences.[5]

For Black and Coward on the contrary, 'experience and identity cannot be seen as the origin of meaning, but as its outcome'.[6] This is the ultimate Saussurean determinism, which sees experience and indeed the individual herself, as a product and function of the institutionalised system of signs. 'Language has a material existence. It defines our possibilities and limitations, it constitutes our subjectivities.'[7] This proposal that meaning does not arise from experience initially strikes most people as running entirely counter to common sense. It is, however, an integral part of semiological approaches which 'decentre the subject', that is, deny there is any unique stable core of personality, human nature, etc. from whose experience meanings could come.

As we have seen, subjectivity is the condition of a social being, aware of her separate existence and the laws of her culture. In contemporary theory of the subject, the process by which this subjectivity develops in children is discussed in terms of psychoanalysis and linguistics; therefore we must look more closely at the psychoanalytic and linguistic account of subject development to be found in the work of Lacan, and at the development of Lacan's ideas by other writers.

PSYCHOANALYSIS

It might well be asked why feminist theory should draw on psychoanalytic concepts. There is no doubt that psychoanalysis as a practice has been very oppressive to women, requiring them to 'adjust' to the stereotype of a passive, powerless and sexually masochistic femininity. Psychoanalysis as a theory, however, is currently popular among feminists because it seems to offer us, through its account of the construction of the self in family relations and the unconscious mind, an understanding of how subordination can be internalised deep in our personalities. Moreover, it is centrally concerned with the forging of sexual identity and with the extreme importance of the sexual in all aspects of mental life. This too has important implications for a politics that stresses sexuality, as feminism does.

Anti-humanism and the Freudian unconscious

The important thing about Freud's work, according to Freudian
semiologists, is that it made possible a revolutionary new concept
of what a human being is. We think of ourselves as stable and
unified entities who 'have' experiences, personalities, sexualities
and so on, but this comfortable 'humanism' is just as illusion.

> For the psychoanalyst the human subject is a complex entity, of
> which the conscious mind is only a small part. Once one has
> accepted this, it becomes impossible to argue that even our
> conscious wishes and feelings originate within a unified self,
> since we can have no knowledge of the possibly unlimited
> unconscious processes which shape our conscious thought.
> Conscious thought, then, must be seen as the overdetermined
> manifestation of a multiplicity of structures which intersect to
> *produce* that unstable constellation the liberal humanists call
> the 'self'. These structures encompass not only unconscious
> sexual desires and unconscious fears and phobias, but also
> conflicting material, social and ideological factors of which we
> are equally unaware. It is this highly complex network of
> conflicting structures, the anti-humanist would argue, that
> produce the subject and its experiences, rather than the other
> way round.[8]

If the monolithic human personality is dethroned by Freud's
discovery of the unconscious, the idea of a natural heterosexuality
is similarly shattered by his findings on psychosexual development. Rather than possessing at birth an essential male or female
nature, with concomitant attraction to the other sex, in Freud's
scheme of things the developing child forges its sexual identity,
a mere and precarious contruct, in the crisis of its relationships
within the family. Thus Freud cleared the way for a radical and
materialist theory of the human subject as something not unified
and static, but created and recreated in a constant process of
conflict and contradiction.

But what has this to do with language? The connection lies in
the notion of a 'symbolic order' or set of meanings which define
culture. In contemporary theory of the subject this symbolic

order is not only to be understood in the same way as a Saussurean *langue*, that is as a system of differences, it is very frequently equated with language itself. Coward and Ellis explain: 'Because all the practices that make up a social totality take place in language, it becomes possible to consider language as the place in which the social individual is constructed.'[9]

It turns out, then, that the term 'subject', designating the social individual in whom semiologists are interested, is a clever pun: for the social individual as well as being the 'subject' of her own perceptions and of the semiologist's enquiry, is a subject in the other sense, 'subject' to the authority and prescriptions of someone or something. That something, according to semiological theory, is precisely the symbolic order, or language. We are all subject to the laws of language, which exist before we are born, and our task in childhood is to insert ourselves into that order so we may secure a place to speak from. If we fail, we become psychotic. Subject development, then, is the process by which the child claims a place in the symbolic order. And that order is reminiscent of Saussure's *langue*, 'outside the individual who can never create or modify it by himself'.[10]

Lacan

Lacan, who as we have seen (Chapter 2) brings the insights of Saussure to bear on Freudian theory, addresses himself to the question of how children take up their place in the symbolic order. He asserts that child development is a several-stage process of 'splitting'. First the child must learn that it is separate from the mother's body; in the mirror stage it recognises its own reflection, further internalising the categories of self and other. Finally, it must learn to separate itself as speaker ('I') from itself as spoken to ('you') or mentioned in the speech of others ('s/he'). Obviously this final splitting of the speaking and the mentioned/addressed subject cannot come about without language, which teaches a whole set of norms and orientations in relation to which the child must locate itself. Language learning is a socialising as well as an individuating process.

From our point of view, Lacan's most important claim is that male and female children enter the symbolic order differently: their relations to language differ. The reason for this difference

lies in the crucial significance of the phallus. To understand wh
Lacan sees the symbolic order as ruled by the phallus, we must g
back to Freud's account of psychosexual development and hi
ideas on civilisation. Freud, it will be recalled, believed tha
children were inherently bisexual; but because civilisatio
requires reproductive sexuality for its continuation, there must b
some process by which the child comes to define itself as male o
female, identifying with one sex and (preferably) desiring th
other. How does this state of affairs come about?

The answer, according to Freud, lies in the child's storm
relations with its parents. Building on clinical observation, Freu
was led to posit an 'Oedipus complex', a stage of development i
which the child entertains feelings of sexual desire for its mothe
and feelings of rage and jealousy toward the father, its rival fo
the mother's affections. This state of affairs is resolved by th
'castration complex', a further stage, in which the phallus plays
crucial symbolic role. It is the castration complex that ac
complishes the differentiation of male and female subjects. Boy
overcome their sexual desire for the mother through their fea
that the father will castrate them, and then go on to identify wit
the father, possessor, like themselves, of the phallus, and beare
of the law. Girls, on the other hand, must recognise that they *ar*
castrated, and will later seek to replace the lost phallus by havin
children. For both sexes, the crucial fact of which they must be
come aware in order to perceive and understand sex different
iation is whether they – and their parents – have the phallus o
not, The law of culture, the symbolic, forces every subject to tak
up a position on one side or the other, having or not-having, eve
if in this non-biologistic account 'Anyone can cross over and in
scribe themselves on the opposite side from that to which they ar
anatomically destined'.[11] In other words, the castration comple
need not always result in 'normal' sexual development (i.e
identification with the subject position of one's anatomical sex
but it must always result in the taking up of one position or th
other.

According to Lacan, the child before its castration complex :
in the order of the Imaginary. Its close relation to its mothe
means that it perceives no lack, no incompleteness, absence
difference or unsatisfied desire. Awareness of these things come
only when a third term, the phallus, is introduced by way of th
castration complex. This precipitates the child's transition fror

the Imaginary to the Symbolic: and it is that transition, together with the meaning of the phallus within it, that we must consider.

Because of its function in the castration complex, the phallus is given two very powerful meanings. One of these is lack, for it symbolises the loss of the mother's body. After the prohibition of incest and threat of castration there can never again be the closeness of mother and child that existed before the introduction of the third term. The other phallic 'meaning' is the Law of patriarchy, a social order in which incest is prohibited and castration threatened by the father. So on one hand the phallus symbolises loss, lack and desire, while on the other it symbolises power and the social order.

For Lacan, it is precisely awareness of lack that impels a child toward language. The idea that words can stand for things can only be grasped when the child has some concept of something missing or absent. Thus there can be no language until the mother/child dyad is broken, and language depends on the introjection of the phallus. This is why Lacan claims that the symbolic order is dominated by the phallus.

ANATOMY AND DESTINY

Feminists have traditionally been very critical of Freudian phallocentrism. They have asked, for instance, why children should conceive the fear of castration, and tried to equate penis envy with girls' envy of the power accorded men in society. So it does perhaps need to be pointed out that castration and penis envy in psychoanalytic theory are meant to be unconscious fantasies, not rationally motivated inferences consciously made by the child. Indeed, they are the inverse of each other: those who have the phallus (boys) nevertheless perceive that others do not, and so they fantasise they will lose it; whereas girls, similarly aware of their own lack and male possession of the phallus, entertain the opposite fantasy. The term *phallus* is meant to denote an object in fantasy, as opposed to *penis* which denotes a real organ, and the Lacanian insists on a careful distinction between the two.

Nevertheless, it can hardly be claimed that the phallus is not, in some sense, the penis. Although we can 'explain' the apparent oddness of castration fears by claiming they are unconscious and not motivated by any occurrence in actual social life (for instance, a real threat of castration by one's father), there is one real-life event that is crucial in triggering anyone's awareness of difference and unconscious fantasies about the phallus. That event is the perception of visible difference. To entertain fears of castration or envy of the penis, a child must somehow know that the genitals of the other sex do not resemble its own. It must register this fact and attach some initial significance to it. In the final analysis then, anatomy cannot be disregarded.

This should not in itself be problematic for feminists, for after all no one has ever denied the anatomical differences between the sexes, nor their obvious importance in determining what our experience of the erotic is going to be like. What does seem problematic is the particular significance give the female genitals in this account. Why should the child, comparing male and female genitals, decide that the boy 'has' something that the girl 'lacks'? Why does the child already have the 'binary opposition' mentality that constructs the world into sets of opposites? Any such presupposition in psychoanalytic theory seems like prima facie evidence for the charge of phallocentrism; (and the case has indeed been argued by Luce Irigaray, whose work we will look at later in this chapter).

The Lacanian commentator Jacqueline Rose replies that the arbitrary interpretation follows from the value of the phallus as a signifier, which is fixed by the symbolic order itself: '... something can only be seen to be missing according to a pre-existing hierarchy of values.... What counts is not the perception but its already assigned meaning...'[12] The locus of explanation returns, therefore, to language and the symbolic, which alone invests difference with significance.

LACANIAN LINGUISTICS: THE SYMBOLIC ORDER

So far, we have been considering the general framework of Lacanian ideas about identity and sexuality. We have seen why Lacan believes children come to language, and why he believes that the order of language is phallic, so that those who do not possess the phallus are marginal to it. We must now examine Lacan's view of language itself.

First, it is important to note a slight confusion which can easily arise around the notion of the symbolic order. Sometimes in Lacanian writing (which is not the same thing as Lacan's writing) this appears to mean the totality of social and cultural practices, including language, while at other times it seems to reduce to language itself, which is alleged to create other cultural practices. The two possibilities invite rather different responses (since the second is more extreme in its determinism than the first) and while we can leave the matter open for the present, the ambiguity should be borne in mind.

Essentially, Lacan's view is a Saussurean one: language is a system of signs defined by their difference from one another. But Lacan differentiates himself from Saussure by pointing out that the signifier is more important than the signified. Rather than representing a signified in a one-to-one correspondence, a signifier refers to the whole inventory of other signifiers from which it is distinct. Only with reference to this chain of associations do we work out what anything means. As Coward and Ellis explain,

> Language is seen to have the dizzying effects of a dictionary: each word, definition by definition, refers to all the others by a series of equivalents; every synonymous substitution is authorised. Language results in tautology, without at any moment having been able to hook onto any signified at all.[13]

The obvious question here is why in that case speakers imagine they are making meaningful remarks that others can interpret, rather than free-associating or playing Chinese Whispers. Lacan meets this objection by speaking of 'points de capiton,' points at which the hypothetically open-ended chain of signifiers actually becomes closed. These 'points de capiton' are contextual phenomena, artefacts of the moment, the situation or the relevant social norms. In Saussurean terminology, they are the limitation imposed by *parole* on *langue*.

At this point we seem to have encountered a puzzle. Lacan (like many other neo-Saussureans) denies any strong indissoluble link between one signifier and one signified (i.e. one form and one meaning) and therefore concludes that meaning is a function of context, intralinguistic associations, social structures and so on. Yet on the other hand he insists that language itself is *constitutive* of the social order; and furthermore, that both language and the order it constitutes pre-exist the individual, whose identity and experience is moulded by the need to insert herself into a preconstituted social reality.

This raises a problem about the phallocentricity of the symbolic order. For if the authority of the phallus, or more generally male authority, is guaranteed neither by inherent anatomical superiority nor by the language, where does it come from? As the third term that breaks up the mother-child dyad, the phallus may always be the spur to language acquisition: but why should it mean what it does mean in the symbolic order? Apparently Lacan has no answer. He asserts what we all know, namely that the symbolic order (taken this time to mean the totality of signifying processes, social, cultural and linguistic) is patriarchal. Inserting oneself in our culture is a matter of submitting to patriarchy. But his theory of language and sexual identity offers no explanation *why* the symbolic order is patriarchal. It can deal with matters of sexual differentiation, but it cannot deal directly with sexual power. Possibly, of course, it was never intended to. But in that case the feminists who have taken it up (Cixous, for example) have been grievously misled as to what its significance is, and they have overestimated its political usefulness.

In fact it seems to me that despite all their disclaimers, despite their awareness of the contextuality of meaning, Lacan and the Lacanians do indulge in a covert Saussurean determinism, which allows meanings to be fixed (though liable to 'slippage') by the linguistic system. For the important concept in Lacanian accounts of language acquisition is the idea of *inserting oneself in a pre-existing order*: and it is difficult to see how anyone could do this unless the order, and the meanings it made available, were fixed and stable, produced outside the individual and enjoined on her as the price of entry into human society.

The neo-Saussureans claim to have improved on Saussure by rejecting the idea of a disembodied system inhering in society and substituting at the theory's centre the actual speaking subject. But it turns out that this subject is constituted precisely by locating herself in relation to a disembodied system that inheres in society. We are all engaged in reproducing the reality language creates: as speaking subjects, we are subject to fixed symbolic laws not of our own making. It is this subjection to symbolic law that Black and Coward have in mind when they claim that meaning produces the individual's experience and not the other way around. And although this view is precisely the opposite of Dale Spender's, it raises, interestingly, exactly the same problems of how meanings can be fixed and whether language does determine reality.

For a number of feminists, Lacan's theory is taken to be an explanation of women's oppression. Women are constructed in the domain of a male sign, and therefore they are, as Lacan put it, 'excluded by the nature of things, which is the nature of words'.[14] The nature of their oppression is once again alienation from the symbolic, being forced to take up a marginal position in the order that circumscribes what it is to be human.

Before looking at the general problems of determinism, control and alienation, we must look at the way in which Lacanian ideas have been used by feminists or at least (since in France the term *feminist* is often seen as a tacit acceptance of the patriarchal male/female dichotomy) by radical women theorists such as the philosopher and critic Julia Kristeva, and the psychoanalyst Luce Irigaray.

JULIA KRISTEVA

Kristeva's work is a development rather than a critique of Lacan's. She believes that femininity is constructed by the mode of entry into the symbolic order, and her major contribution, so far as the subject of this book is concerned, is to spell out the radical rejection of anatomy as destiny entailed by Lacanian linguistics, together with the implications of that rejection for feminists.

Kristeva discusses the pre-Oedipal Imaginary stage before language acquisition, in an interesting way. She suggests that before the symbolic order there is a *semiotic order* linked to oral and anal drives which flow across the child. The 'pulsions' of these drives are gathered in a *chora* (which means, approximately, a receptacle). Later, when the child takes up a position in the symbolic order as a result of the castration complex, the contents of the chora will be repressed, but its influence will nevertheless be discernible in linguistic discourse through rhythm, intonation, gaps, meaninglessness and general

textual disruption. Indeed some discourses, like art, poetry and
madness, draw on the semiotic rather than the symbolic aspects
of language.

For Kristeva, there is a possibility of choice about what subject
position the child takes up (male, fully integrated into the
symbolic, or female, marginal to it). It is not a matter of biology
but of identification with one parent or the other. Thus
femininity, defined as marginality to the symbolic order, is open
to men as well as women. Anyone taking up a feminine subject
position retains strong links with the pre-Oedipal mother figure
and their language shows the influence of the chora to a marked
degree. It is this ability of the chora to break through rational
discourse that gives, for instance, French modernist poetry its
distinctive quality:

> The modernist poem, with its abrupt shifts, ellipses, breaks
> and apparent lack of logical construction is a kind of writing in
> which the rhythms of the body and the unconscious have
> managed to break through the strict, rational defences of
> conventional social meaning. Since Kristeva sees such meaning
> as the structure that sustains the whole of the symbolic order –
> that is, all human social and cultural institutions – the break
> down of symbolic language in modernist poetry comes to
> prefigure for her a total *social* revolution.[15]

Here we see how important is Kristeva's emphasis on femininity as
non-biological – for the poets she deals with – Mallarmé and
Lautréamont – were, of course, men.

But if it is one's position in the symbolic that makes one
masculine or feminine, the identification of these categories with
biological maleness and femaleness is exposed as a trick.
Femininity and womanhood are not the same, but patriarchy
makes them appear identical. And because women, inaccurately
but unproblematically identified with feminine subjects, are
marginal to the symbolic order, they come to represent the
boundary between symbolic order and imaginary chaos. As Tori
Moi observes,

> It is this position which has enabled male culture sometimes to
> vilify women as representing darkness and chaos – the chaos of
> the *chora* or of the imaginary, one might add – and sometimes

to elevate them as the representatives of a higher and purer nature than men.[16]

Kristeva sees different kinds of feminism as embodying different attitudes to the symbolic. Liberal, equal-rights feminism demands for women an equal rather than a marginal place in the symbolic. Radical feminism extols the distinctively feminine, which means it rejects the value placed on the symbolic altogether. A further stage, which Kristeva speaks of as the 'third generation', would reject the very opposition of male and female as metaphysical, and attack the whole notion of sexual, or even general, identity.

We have not yet got beyond the radical stage, and it remains necessary both to reclaim and to proclaim the feminine within language. But unless we are aware that the masculine/feminine dichotomy is itself to be questioned, our struggle will not get beyond the inverted sexism which comes from keeping the same old categories and merely swapping round the positions of those who occupy them. Because in Kristeva's theory language indeed 'defines our possibilities and limitations...constitutes our subjectivities', there can be no escape from the authoritarian and phallocentric symbolic order. The alternative to the symbolic is psychosis. But the order can be subverted from within, and that subversion for Kristeva is a revolutionary act.

LUCE IRIGARAY

Luce Irigaray is a psychoanalyst trained in the Lacanian framework. During the 1970s, however, she mounted a relentless critique of Lacan, focusing especially on questions of femininity and language. She was expelled from Lacan's school after the publication in 1974 of her book *Speculum de l'autre femme*. Irigaray's main objection to Lacan is that his system cannot admit any kind of plurality, either in sexuality or in language (which for her, as for him, is closely linked with sexuality). This leads to women's otherness or difference being denied, and their mere oppositeness asserted.

To Lacan's famous pronouncement, 'the unconscious is structured like a language', Irigaray asks 'which language?' For

Lacan there can only be one, and women's relation to it is negative. For Irigaray, women have a language of their own, related to their sexuality and imagination. This language is not merely repressed, like the signifiers of Kristeva's *chora*, but actually *suppressed*, denied existence at any level. Irigaray believes that this suppression, and therefore the question of language, is fundamental to patriarchy,

> The question of language is closely allied to that of feminine sexuality. For I do not believe that language is universal, or neutral with regard to the difference of the sexes. In the face of language, constructed and maintained by men only, I raise the question of the specificity of a feminine language; of a language which would be adequate for the body, sex and the imagination...of the woman. A language which presents itself as universal, and which is in fact produced by men only, is this not what maintains the alienation and exploitation of women in and by society?[17]

What Lacan conceptualises as a lack in woman, Irigaray regards as difference. Women's language, if it were not suppressed, would be different from men's in two major ways. The first (which reminds one of the feminist-folklinguistic rejection of logic and the complete sentence) is syntactic: 'it has nothing to do with the syntax we have used for centuries, namely...subject, predicate or subject, verb, object. The female sexuality is not unifiable.'[18] The second also reflects the alleged plurality of feminine sexuality, and relates to meaning:

> There will always be a plurality in feminine language. And it will not even be the Freudian 'pun', i.e. a superimposed hierarchy of meaning, but the fact that at each moment there are always for women at least two meanings, without one being able to decide which meaning prevails, which is 'on top' or 'underneath', which conscious or 'repressed'. For a feminine language would undo the unique meaning, the proper meaning of words, of nouns, which still regulates discourse.[19]

This rejection of semantic determinacy (about which I shall have more to say in the next chapter, for it is of paramount importance) is a challenge not only to Lacan, but more important, to Saussure and the whole apparatus of structuralism. Where words have more than one meaning, and no meaning is more basic than any other, the one-to-one correspondence between signifier and signified which guarantees the unity of the sign is broken down. Irigaray is obviously aware what a drastic step she is taking here, for she remarks that Lacan never went far enough: 'There was I think one further step to take: to question linguistic theory itself, viz. structuralism, and more generally, any formalism.'[20]

Unlike Lacan, then, Irigaray specifically rejects linguistic determinism, and holds that there need be no fixed order of meanings for the subject to enter. At present, however, males do have control over the language and its meanings. This is not necessarily anything mysterious: men simply silence women, often (as in Irigaray's own case) by quite literally taking away their platform. 'Women are not allowed to speak, otherwise they challenge the monopoly of discourse and of theory exerted by men.'[21] This silence is all too obvious, Irigaray claims, in the differing behaviour of male and female schizophrenics. Whereas men typically produce linguistic symptoms for the analyst to work on, women schizophrenics find it more difficult to articulate their illness, and suffer it therefore in the form of psychosomatic pain.

PROBLEMS: LANGUAGE AND THE BODY

In her concern for a 'women's language' Irigaray is very typical of many feminists in France and, increasingly, in Britain and the USA. Influenced by the Lacanian dictum that 'women are excluded by the nature of things, which is the nature of words', these women make a strong connection between language and sexuality, language and the body, and they have urged that writers take up the quest for a signifying system appropriate to the feminine body. Such a language would be able to express women's experience: whereas all current western discourse presents, as Irigaray phrases it, 'a certain isomorphism with the masculine sex'. The rallying-cry is 'write your body': that is, women are urged to find a form of writing in which the specific rhythms of the female body and the conflicting forces within the female unconscious can come out.

So it is worth considering whether the idea of a relation between language and the body is a useful one. To some feminists it appears, on the contrary, as dangerous biologism that plays into the hands of the patriarchs. This argument is convincingly presented in the first number of a French theoretical journal, *Questions féministes*:

> To advocate a 'woman's language' . . . seems to us . . . illusory. . . . It is at times said that women's language is closer to the body, to sexual pleasure, to direct sensations and so on, which means that the body could express itself directly without special mediation and that, moreover this closeness to the body and to nature would be subversive. In our opinion, there is no such thing as a direct relation to the body. To advocate a direct relation to the body is therefore not subversive because it is equivalent to denying the reality and the strength of social mediations, the very same ones that oppress us in our bodies. At most, one would advocate a different socialisation of the body, but without searching for a true and eternal nature, for this search takes us away from the most effective struggle against the socio-historical contexts in which human beings are and will always be trapped.[22]

Or as Mary Jacobus pithily puts it, 'if anatomy is not destiny, still less can it be language'.[23]

Even leaving aside the problem of language and the body, however, the psychoanalytic framework itself appears to raise serious problems. Some of these are the same problems we have seen in the work of Shirley Ardener and Dale Spender, but others are more specific to the context of psychoanalysis. It is possible, of course, to take an entirely sceptical view of Freud and all his works. Many systems of talking about mental life do not give the same place as Freud does to sexuality and even to the unconscious: and as the materialist feminist Christine Delphy remarks, why should anyone swallow whole the 'extravagant claim of psychoanalysis to be, not a system of interpretation of subjectivity, but subjectivity itself. I will not accept that objecting to the theory of psychoanalysis is synonymous with disinterest in its object.'[24] In other words, Freudian theory is not to be taken as a given: we are entitled to ask if it is correct. Such empiricism may be foreign to the Lacanians, but it certainly was not foreign to

Freud, whose observations stood or fell by the quality of clinical evidence he was able to produce in support of them.

If we want to take Lacanian and Freudian ideas critically on board, however, two questions arise immediately. The first of these concerns the place of the social in child development. For it seems quite obvious that the construction of what in our culture passes for masculinity or femininity is not simply a drama that unfolds within the child's private mental life. It is also to some extent a matter of what feminists have long referred to as 'conditioning'. Studies have repeatedly shown that girls and boys are treated quite differently from birth, and that appropriate behaviours are explicitly taught. This socialisation may have nothing to do with sexuality *per se* (though I shall argue in a moment that even this would be an over-simplification) but it is extremely relevant to the social category of gender.

This is not to suggest that a crude social conditioning model must be superior to a psychoanalytic account of child development. On the contrary, the importance of infantile sexuality and of mental life in general, can hardly be denied even by theorists implacably opposed to Freud. The point is that neither account will do on its own. We cannot leave socialisation out. We need to know what part it plays in child development and also how it relates to the psycho-sexual processes described by psychoanalysis. For instance, are the Oedipus and castration complexes human universals, or are they specific to some particular kind of family organisation (e.g. the nuclear family)? If women did not bear sole responsibility for childcare, would loss of the maternal body retain the status Lacan accords it, or will the fact that women *bear* children always dictate a close psychological identification between mother and child?

The second problem relates to language. We need to know, for instance, how Lacanian accounts of language acquisition can be related to the large body of work on the subject by linguists and psychologists. As matters stand, there is little evidence that children's acquisition of language is significantly affected by their sex. Nor does there seem to be much evidence for the alleged marginality of women as speakers and writers, which is something I shall return to. Indeed, it is difficult to see how, in the Lacanian or Kristevan framework, one would evaluate the theory that feminine subjects are marginal to the symbolic order: if femininity is defined as marginality, and a writer's identification as feminine can only be inferred from her/his writing itself, the theory seems endlessly circular and impossible to check. (It is only fair to point out that Lacan and Kristeva would not accept this as an objection to their theories, for theirs is an anti-empiricist tradition: nevertheless it strikes me and many other linguists as a problem.)

There is one final, explicitly political problem which can usefully be mentioned here. As we have seen, psychoanalytic and anti-humanist approaches downgrade the notion of 'experience' which has previously been (and in the Anglo-American tradition, remains) central to feminist politics. But in denying that feminism can be the politics of experience, it could be argued that the semiologists miss, or even deliberately conceal, an important difference between women and men. This is precisely the experience women have of being sexually oppressed by men. It would be wholly unreasonable to argue, I think, that awareness of one's subjection (in the case of women) or power (in the case of men) could make *no difference* to one's sexuality.

But if we accept that one's actual status as powerful/powerless sexually is an important formative experience, what becomes of the dogma that men too can be feminine subjects and feminists? It has to be discarded at once, for power in society is as a matter of established fact assigned not on the basis of identification choices, but simply on the basis of biological sex. And there is thus no choice about whether you are an oppressor or one of the oppressed.

In the final analysis, then, it seems to me that radical feminists must be intensely suspicious of theories that invalidate experience and make the subordinate status of women a consequence of something other than their mere womanhood. These theories all too often turn out to be a cover for the role of men in upholding male power, or else an apology for the participation of men in the feminist movement. In other words, a wholly theoretical and non-biological concept of gender, sexuality and so on makes it too easy not to emphasise the real power differences between the sexes. Diana Leonard makes the following acute observation:

> It is always a joy to hear men . . . asserting that which side you are on is not a question of whether you exert or suffer oppression, but of what values you hold. And it is classic to turn the accusation of sexism and biologism back on the

victims, as if hostility to the oppressor is the same as hostility to the oppressed, and as if it were radical and revolutionary feminists who had invented the crazy idea that having or not having a penis/phallus should be the source of significant differences in the way in which society treats 'individuals'.[25]

Psychoanalytic approaches to sex difference and women's oppression have undoubtedly introduced stimulating ideas to the feminist debate, but in evaluating them we must bear Diana Leonard's warning in mind.

It will be clear by now that although the Ardeners, Spender, Black and Coward, Irigaray and Kristeva diverge in important ways from one another, they all subscribe to some degree of determinism, to the idea that men control language and (especially) to the notion that women are alienated from it to a degree that men are not. They stress the basic inauthenticity of women's language at present, the difficulties women have in talking about their experience, or sexuality. They trace back to this linguistic disadvantage important elements of women's subjection, and recommend either subversion of symbolic language or the forging of an authentically female code.

In Chapter 8 I shall take issue with this view of women, language and oppression. I shall be asking how, and to what extent, the resources of language are used to construct and/or maintain the power of men over women.

8 Beyond Alienation: An Integrational Approach to Women and Language

> I have come to believe over and over again that
> what is most important to me must be spoken, made
> verbal and shared, even at the risk of having it
> bruised and misunderstood. That the speaking
> profits me, beyond any other effect.
>
> *Audre Lorde*

> The central indeterminacy of all communication is
> indeterminacy of what is meant.
>
> *Roy Harris*

This chapter articulates a view of language rather different from any we have looked at so far. In it I am critical of those theorists who claim that men control language and language controls us, whether or not that claim is dressed up in the complexities of psychoanalysis. On the one hand, theories of alienation and inauthenticity seem to me misguided because they locate us in a linguistic utopia which never has existed, and never will exist: on the other, I find them politically dubious because they are remote from the lived experience of women, and indeed reject the validity of much of that experience.

I do not deny that books such as Dale Spender's have had a very positive response from women who felt they recognised the processes of muting and misunderstanding discussed in *Man Made Language*. What I do deny is the idea that, in order to explain these things, we have to resort to notions of alienation, male control, negative semantic space and negative entry into the symbolic, female inauthenticity (a new and pernicious sort of female inadequacy) and the creaking apparatus of linguistic determinism. These notions mystify language and demoralise women. The only feminist theory they engender is an arid, intellectuals-only theory of no hope.

Marks and de Courtivron, in their introduction to a collection of French writings, admit that semiology, though stimulating, may turn out to be unproductive politically:

'Within the structuralist vision...there is no liberation from oppression, but there is an immense energy released by the attempts to analyze and demystify the structures that determine and oppress us.'[1]

Is this really enough?

Some feminists believe it is not. In 1976, at a conference on patriarchy, a paper was read which gave an account of Lacanian psychoanalysis and its relevance to feminism.[2] Published alongside that paper and others from the conference was a critique written later by the Dalston Study Group. This critique, titled 'Was the patriarchy conference "patriarchal"?', emphasised the hostility and dissatisfaction produced at the conference by the psychoanalysis paper, and pointed to the source of that dissatisfaction:

'It felt ironical, then, to arrive at a women's conference and feel defined negatively in relation to it; to listen to papers being read about women's silence and women having no social language, which itself made us passive and silent.'[3]

The Dalston Study Group objected not only to the content of the paper but to the language it was written in. In their opinion, it was exactly that sort of language women found most alienating: the authors of the psychoanalysis paper had reproduced the process by which academics are so often able to exclude less privileged groups. As the Dalston women put it,

The language used ... had the effect of *making* large numbers of women feel inadequate, stupid or angry...the process we identify in education as a process of socialisation which often makes women, blacks, working-class people, etc., unconfident and suspicious of intellectual work, and makes them doubt the strength and potential of their own language. It also perpetuates the split between the undervalued day-to-day language of such groups...and the impoverished depersonal ised analytical language of intellectuals.[4]

In this chapter I want to explore the possibility that the linguistic mechanisms used to oppress women are like the one being alluded to here, rather than the ones discussed in Chapte 7. The first puzzle that needs to be solved before we can look a women's day-to-day language and the strategies used to devalue i is this: why do the pontifications of intellectuals, and particularl those intellectuals whose business it is to talk about language concern themselves so little with everyday speech and communication? It is quite obvious, for instance, that linguistic has nothing much to say about these things (the devaluing o ordinary language is institutionalised in the split between *langu* and *parole*, competence and performance) and from thi shortcoming we get many of the misconceptions on which theorie of alienation are built. So as a preliminary to my analysis o women's oppression through language, I propose to examine the linguist's conceptions of language, meaning and communicatio and to criticise them on a number of grounds.

WHAT DO WE MEAN BY 'LANGUAGE'?

It has often been pointed out that the word *language* has at leas two meanings. It can refer to a general human faculty lik 'cognition' or 'sense perception', in which case it is a fairly genera and abstract term; alternatively it can refer to a particular entit like 'English' or Swahili'. In a great deal of lay and theoretical tal about language, these two senses are not very rigorously kep apart.

In addition to this possible confusion, there are two ways i which scholars can look at languages. On the one hand, 'Englis may be regarded as an institution, on the other, as an object.

If language is an institution, the task of the scholar must be t codify its conventions in things like the dictionary (fo conventions of pronunciation and meaning), the grammar book the style sheet, the thesaurus and so on. Some languages are mor thoroughly codified than others. The ministry of Dutch culture i Belgium, for instance, regularly issues a definitive account c what words and constructions are to count as proper usage for the Flemish population. Civil servants and university students are expected to comply with ministerial directives in their use of language. Although English is not subject to a centralised authority of this kind, nevertheless it has many of the trappings of an institution: dictionaries, books of standard usage, etc., whose prestige is very high.

Those who subscribe to the institutional view of language are quite clear that 'English' is a cultural artefact which needs to be regulated and protected from abuse (for instance, debasement by foreigners and the lower orders). 'Language' is just a kind of shorthand for 'correct usage' or 'the language of the most educated/privileged speakers'. Communication is taken for granted: it is assumed that people know how to communicate and only need to be taught the most elegant way of doing it.

Feminist reformists like Miller and Swift, whose targets are the 'institutional' trappings of language (the journalistic style manual and the editor's guidelines) appeal to these same notions of clarity, elegance and accuracy. They differ from the sort of person who writes to the newspapers about bad grammar/sloppy speech only in their ideas of what *is* correct usage. For them accuracy means including women.

Linguistics pretends to be above this kind of judgement, which is selective, prescriptive and therefore unscientific. For the linguist, language is not an institution but an object, to be abstracted for observational purposed from the circumstances in which it is used and the people who use it. Whether it is Saussurean sign-system, where terms enter into relations with each other and no relations with anything outside, or the idealised grammar rules of transformational models, the linguist's language has no users and no uses. The institutions which grow up around it are ignored (though it would be quite feasible to study them *without* descending to prescriptivism) and the question of communication is sidestepped. Studying language as an object rather than an institution or a process causes linguistics to exclude much that is not only interesting but crucial.

WHAT DO WE MEAN BY 'MEANING'?

Even if communication were on the linguistics agenda, it is

doubtful that anything illuminating could be said about it within the orthodox framework. To ask about communication, after all, is to ask how hearers ascribe meaning to what speakers say: and the linguist has a very simplistic notion of meaning.

In her autobiography, Simone de Beauvoir describes a private world of prelinguistic experience, which words, when she comes to use them, can render only imperfectly. 'White was only rarely totally white, and the blackness of evil was relieved by lighter touches; I saw greys and half-tones everywhere. Only as soon as I tried to define their muted shades, I had to use words, and found myself in a world of bony-structured concepts.'[5] Having admitted the necessity for language, however, de Beauvoir fell into the opposite error of assuming there was no meaning outside the rigid definitions given her by parents and relatives.

> As I had failed in my efforts to think without recourse to language...I assumed that this was an exact equivalent of reality; I was encouraged in this misconception by the grown-ups, whom I took to be the sole depositaries of absolute truth: when they defined a thing, they expressed its substance, in the sense in which one expresses the juice from a fruit. So that I could conceive of no gap into which error might fall between the word and its object; that is why I submitted myself uncritically to the Word, without examining its meaning, even when circumstances inclined me to doubt its truth.[6]

Both these ideas are presented as the unsophisticated theories of a child, and both make the same mistake: they assume that words express private experience perfectly, and that there can be no argument about what they mean. Adults, on the other hand, rarely believe in practice in absolute truth and exhaustive definition. They learn that words may easily lie and distort, that they are vague, ambiguous and sometimes inadequate. When they fail, of course, there are always other words with which we may attempt clarification: even this will never be a complete success. The representation by words of experience is partial in all senses of that term. This is a truism of everyday communication that linguistics has never come to terms with.

The model of communication which has dominated western philosophy and linguistics is, as Roy Harris points out, essentially *telementational*. Language is envisaged as a means by which a speaker can transfer a thought from her own mind to her hearer's.[7] This is possible because the speaker and hearer share a code, a set of correspondences between forms and meanings. Given something she wishes to convey, a speaker is able to select the form associated with her chosen concept; the resulting utterance will be decoded by the hearer in the same way, by matching it up to a concept – the same concept – in her own mind.

But this can only work if there really is a unique one-to-one correspondence between forms (words, say) and meanings, a correspondence reproduced in the mind of everyone who speaks the same language. If that correspondence were absent, we could never be sure we had really understood what anyone said, since the incoming acoustic signal would not necessarily evoke the same concept which had spawned it in the speaker's discourse originally. Linguistics assumes that there is such a one-to-one correspondence, and that the unique pairings of forms and meanings in each language are precisely what the linguist has to work out. Hence the Saussurean sign, in which form (signifier) and meaning (signified) are so fused together that dividing them is impossible. Orthodox linguistic models hold

> that the ideal community will have a language in which all the basic units must be determinate and all the rules which govern their combinations and interpretations must be determinate. For otherwise there is no possibility of a common codebook for the whole community . . . the expressions of a language in some sense have to be determinate in respect both of 'form' and of 'meaning'. That is to say, there must be fixed rules. . .for assigning the correct interpretation to any expression.[8]

It is this assumption that Harris labels 'the language myth'. It leads to the uncritical submission to the word recalled by Simone de Beauvoir: it leads to linguistic determinism and the tyranny of the sign. Fortunately for human communication, this model of meaning is false.

Harris suggests replacing the language myth with a 'demythologised' or 'integrational' linguistics which would embody quite a different way of looking at language and a radically different theory of meaning. Integrational linguistics would acknowledge two crucial things about language. The first of these is that language cannot be sealed off from every other form of social behaviour, nor abstracted from the dimensions of time and space to which all such behaviour is inevitably subject. As Harris says, 'Human beings inhabit a communicational space which is not neatly compartmentalised into language and non-language.'[9] Locating speech events in time and space (which means abolishing the Saussurean dichotomies of synchrony/diachrony and *langue/parole*) is extremely important to an integrational analysis. By paying attention to the whole context in which speech occurs, the analyst would be spared the necessity of postulating invariant correspondences of form and meaning: she could allow what we all know, that words are used and understood differently by different speakers at different times and in different situations, and she could refer to the specifics of context in order to explain that variation.

The second thing is that language-using is a creative process. There is pretty well no limit to the novel situations humans may encounter, and therefore the communicational demands which may be made on them are almost limitless. To meet those demands, speakers and hearers engage in a constant renewal of language. They employ words in a flexible, innovative and often playful way, and are creative in their interpretations of other speakers. In a linguistics which takes account of this, Harris observes, 'It would no longer be necessary to reduce speaker and hearer to mere automata, handling pre-packaged messages in accordance with mechanical rules.'[10] The orthodox linguistic view of meaning sees language users looking up meanings in some internalised dictionary. The integrational view, on the contrary, sees them creating meaning in specific contexts, negotiating where necessary in order to achieve as fully as possible their communicational aims.

In practice, indeterminacy of meaning is acknowledged by structuralist and post-structuralist writers in their notion of 'deconstruction', a sort of reading that challenges established forms of criticism by denying that the 'true meaning' of any text can ever be arrived at. Deconstruction is a process of making text yield a multiplicity of meanings; none is counted more basic than any other, and there is no end to the process. Such open endedness is exactly what the integrationalist approach to language proclaims. But for an integrationalist it is quite baffling to find practitioners of deconstruction claiming that creativity i made possible by the existence of a decontextualised and fixed set of signs, *langue*. This ossified structure, with determinacy of form and meaning at its core, is exactly what integrationalists would want to dispense with on the grounds that it denies all creativity and thus renders the sort of communication typical of human activity utterly incomprehensible.

This dispute is not trivial for feminists. Rejecting the notion of *langue* and the determinate sign means rejecting the feminist positions set out in Chapter 6. There can be no linguistic determinism, no control of meaning by men, no privilege of the phallus as signifier and thus no alienation.

MEANING, UNDERSTANDING AND ALIENATION

We may now return to the experience described by Simone de Beauvoir: 'I saw greys and half-tones everywhere. Only as soon as I tried to define their muted shades, I had to use words, and I found myself in a world of bony-structured concepts.'[11] This frustration at being unable to make language express the exact nuances of experience is something we have already encountered in women's own testimony: 'Sometimes when I am talking to people I really feel at a loss for words. . . . A vast number of the words I use all the time to describe my experience are not really describing it at all.'[12] Audre Lorde, a poet, notes that we speak of our experience only 'at the risk of having it bruised and misunderstood'.[13] Difficulty in finding words and difficulty in being understood are often spoken of by women as signs of their alienation, the proof that 'this is the oppressors language' with meanings and limits defined by men. The solution is to create a new language in which women can express their meanings and be understood.

But if we accept the idea that meaning is complex, plural and ultimately perhaps impossible to pin down, the new language solution appears utopian. There will never be a perfect fit between private experience and linguistic expression, and there will never be perfect mutual understanding. Sociologists of language have long been familiar with the idea that participants in any kind of talk take for granted a degree of comprehension which, when you look more closely at the interaction, cannot ever be quite justified. Thus the problems of expressing oneself and being understood are not exclusively women's problems. They are built into all interaction and affect all speakers. Which is not to say that women do not suffer to a greater degree than men: for the causes of their particular problems, however, I think it is necessary to consider the whole social situation of women and men, and not just their relative positions in an abstract symbolic order.

The notion that perfect mutual understanding – telepathy – is not the normal or the ideal outcome of speaking, frightens and confuses many people. It is clear that without the indeterminacy that stops us communicating telepathically we would not be able to adapt our language to the novel situations we need it for: imperfect communication is the price we pay for a creative and flexible symbolic system. But this important insight frequently meets with a great deal of resistance. If we cannot ever really understand each other, are we not trapped in our own private worlds with no hope of making contact? And is this not the ultimate nightmare of alienation?

This fear, and the comforting certainty that perfect understanding *is* possible, goes very deep. For instance, a well known myth of human prehistory refers to a time when humans did understand each other perfectly, and this understanding conferred enormous power on them. God not unnaturally saw that power as a threat and destroyed it by destroying the unity of human language.

> And the Lord said, Behold, the people is one, and they have all one language; and this they begin to do: and now nothing will be restrained from them, which they have imagined to do. Go to, let us go down, and there confound their language, that they may not understand each other's speech. So the Lord scattered them abroad from thence upon the face of all the earth.[14]

The perfect understanding which supposedly results from 'speaking the same language' is seen here as an essential prerequisite for any kind of collective action. God, in replacing linguistic unity with linguistic diversity, undermined the power of the builders. Feminists have their own version of the Tower of

Babel story. They feel that men have undermined women by confounding their language, the language of their bodies, their unconscious, their desire or their experience. In order to act together, an authentic language of women must be forged. If there is no common language, there can be no true collective action.

I do not feel, however, that the view of meaning I have put forward excludes the possibility of collective action, nor does it negate the communication that obviously *does* occur between individuals. Rather, it says that if we are ever to understand the nature of collective action and interpersonal communication, we must first acknowledge its inherent difficulties and limitations. Until we do acknowledge that communication is to some extent an everyday triumph, until we get rid of our fantasies of what it never can be, we can hardly study it at all, but will be content either to avoid the issue or to take it for granted.

Where does this leave the feminist theories of language and oppression we have discussed in this book? I suggest that it leaves us with three propositions corresponding to the three feminist axioms of linguistic determinism, male control and female alienation.

1. Linguistic determinism is a myth. Where there is no determinacy, there can be no determinism. In a system where language and linguistic acts are integrated with non-linguistic acts and social life generally, language can be only one of the multiple determinants of any individual's perceptions and experience. An important determinant it may be, but it cannot be privileged to the extent that both Saussurean and Whorfian theories privilege it.

2. Male control over meaning is an impossibility. No group has it in their power to fix what expressions of a language will mean, because meanings cannot be fixed, and interpretation will be dependent not on the authority of some vast internal dictionary, but on the creative and ultimately idiosyncratic use of past experience and present context.

Learning to communicate and to participate in social life is something which both male and female children do. They do it by actively interacting with their environment and the people in it, and thus they construct – rather than learn – meanings that are highly contextualised, dependent on that environment and those people, subject (as the environment is) to variation and to change.

It would be very surprising if this learning process did not exhibit sex-linked differences. Girls and boys, after all, are very specifically socialised into female and male gender roles; one would expect them to construct meanings which were different not only idiosyncratically, because each individual has a different experience, but more generally, because in patriarchal societies males and females are allowed a different range of experiences. Perhaps, then, we may talk to some extent of male and female meanings. But we cannot speak of women being socialised into male meanings, or of both sexes being socialised into patriarchal meanings (except in the sense that their experience is one of living under patriarchy). Meanings have to be constructed by the individual language user (in this way language is radically unlike, say, folk tales or table manners) and any child who does not learn to construct meanings out of her own interaction with the world cannot be said to possess language at all.

3.   Female alienation from language does not exist in the form postulated by the theories we have considered (it should not be denied either in theory or in practice that many women do feel extremely alienated in some modes of language use). Since language is a flexible and renewable resource, and since girls must come to grips with it as their socialisation proceeds, there is no reason in principle why language cannot express the experience of women to the same extent that it expresses the experience of men.

In saying this, however, I do not wish to deny that women have real problems in speaking and being heard. Although I reject the usual explanations of them, I believe that the means do exist for men to oppress, silence and marginalise women through language. The sources of silence and oppression are what I want to turn to now.

LINGUISTIC OPPRESSION: WHAT IT IS THAT MEN CONTROL

One consequence of the integrational approach to language is that the linguist has to take seriously the fact that languages are not used in a social and political vacuum, i.e. she must recognise the institutional aspects of language I have already mentioned in this chapter.

In every society, one finds laws, rituals and institutions which regulate language (especially its more public modes) in particular ways. As we saw in Chapter 3, it is not always easy to separate these 'metalinguistic' or 'discursive' practices from language proper, since there is a constant interaction between the two. From an integrational standpoint it is not even worth trying to exclude the metalinguistic: institutional phenomena are part of what the linguist must be concerned with.

If we look closely at the regulatory mechanisms which grow up around languages, it is clear that they are rather closely connected with the power structures of their society. The institutions that regulate language use in our own society, and indeed those of most societies, are deliberately oppressive to women. Men control them, not in the rather mystical sense that they are said to control meaning, by making esoteric semantic rules or possessing the vital signifier, but simply because it is the prerogative of those with economic and political power to set up and regulate important social institutions.

Language, the human faculty and communication channel, may belong to everyone; because of the crucial part it plays in human cognition and development, it cannot be appropriated. But *the* language, the institution, the apparatus of ritual, value judgement and so on, does not belong to everyone equally. It can be controlled by a small elite. As Trevor Pateman remarks,

Language, though the socially produced means of thought, is not socially controlled. Increasingly control over the development of language and its use is held by state institutions, including mass-media and monopolistic private enterprise, as in journalism and advertising.... The semiologists have sometimes failed to appreciate the possibility and existence of class or other minority control over language.[15]

If we acknowledge the importance of institutional control, the crucial question is: how is male control over metalinguistic processes manifested, and what effects does it have on women? I want to consider this now, and true to my integrational aims I shall not be limiting my remarks to linguistic phenomena alone.

It is impossible to understand the practices that regulate women's relation to language except with reference to gender roles and regulatory mechanisms is general.

'HIGH LANGUAGE' AND WOMEN'S SILENCE

Cora Kaplan, in a short but influential essay, makes a point that has since become the received view about women's oppression by linguistic institutions; the point is that women are denied access to the most influential and prestigious registers of language in a particular culture.[16] That is to say, everything defined as 'high' language (for instance, political and literary registers, the register of public speaking and especially ritual – religious, legal or social) is also defined as *male* language. Kaplan observes,

> The prejudice seems persistent and irrational unless we acknowledge that control of high language is a crucial part of the power of dominant groups, and understand the refusal of access to public language is one of the major forms of the oppression of women within a social class as well as in trans-class situations.[17]

If it is in their relation to high language that women are linguistically disadvantaged, it seems that we must ask three questions: *what* are the registers that men control, *how* do they gain and keep control of those registers, and *why* does male control constitute a disadvantage for women? I propose to explore these questions by focusing on particular areas of language use and linguistic control. First there is the area of written language and women's relation to it. An investigation of this shows how a denial of language can constitute a denial of knowledge and of certain kinds of consciousness. Then, there is the problem of bureaucratic/institutional language. Recent work on interethnic communication demonstrates how very tightly controlled norms are used to define subordinate groups as inadequate communicators (and thus to *make* them inadequate). Finally, we must examine the exclusion of women from public and ritual speech, investigating the extent to which femininity has been produced as incompatible with the sphere of rhetoric.

WOMEN AND LITERACY

Literacy – the ability to read and write – may seem to us a 'natural' concomitant of all language, but in fact it is a relatively recent technology (6000 years old, whereas human culture is at least 30,000 years old) and like most technologies, male-dominated throughout its history. The definitive account of women's relation to literacy has yet to be written, but research currently available gives feminists food for thought.

Of the approximately 800 million illiterates in the world today, the majority are women: indeed the higher a country's over-all rate of illiteracy, the wider the gap between women and men.[18] Literacy has been a mostly-male phenomenon in the developed world historically even when it meant being able to write your own mother tongue; in the centuries when it meant knowledge of a superordinate 'learned' language such as Latin, classical Arabic or Sanskrit, literacy was effectively a sex-exclusive marker.[19]

Why are women so frequently illiterate? The short answer is, of course, that where the education required to produce literacy is not available to everyone automatically (and indeed compulsorily), women do not get it. Poor countries and poor families cannot afford to educate children whose destiny is marriage and domestic labour rather than the bureaucratic, commercial, scholarly and scientific work literacy facilitates. However, there must be more to it than this, since although the same argument applies to working-class and peasant men (whose work does not demand literacy any more than women's does) they are more likely than their wives and sisters to be able to read. The exclusion of women from education and thus from literacy is not simply a side-effect of economic circumstances, but a way of keeping the female in her place – dependent and domesticated, both physically and mentally. We can see this more clearly if we examine what one expert has to say about the difference literacy makes to a person's attitudes.

> the more literate people are, the more willing they are to accept and work for improvements in their societies. Their sense of 'personal efficacy' is increased: that is, they gain confidence that they are able to do something about their own lives. . . . They become more willing to reason for themselves, less willing to take opinions on authority.[20]

It is evident that the maintenance of compliant femininity is threatened by these qualities. Literacy has always been associated with democracy and with modernisation in less developed countries, and just as the ruling class fear these things if a literate proletariat emerges, men defend their own power by denying women this crucial democratising technology.

In western European culture, women have been literate in their own language for many years. What they missed through being denied access to education was literacy in Latin, the language of learning and culture in western Europe. This effectively insulated women from a great deal of knowledge, and possibly also from a particular, and particularly influential, way of thinking. Ong remarks,

> Writing . . . serves to separate and distance the knower and the known and thus to establish objectivity. . . . Learned Latin effects even greater objectivity by establishing knowledge in a medium insulated from the emotion charged depths of one's mother-tongue, thus reducing interference from the human lifeworld and making possible the exquisitely abstract world of medieval scholasticism and the new mathematical modern science.[21]

This does not mean, of course, that science and mathematics are inherently male discourses founded upon a male language. Girls have proved their abilities in Latin and in science. What is important is that these discourses were *historically* masculine and specifically denied to women. Ultimately it is that history which determines women's current relation to science, even if rather indirectly and obscurely. Saussure was wrong in supposing that the speaker/writer has no awareness of history at all: most of us *are* aware of linguistic tradition, custom and practice, and may well be insecure or tentative users of discourses we (or our ancestors) had to fight to get into. This has nothing to do with the language itself and everything to do with the way we were defined in relation to it.

To sum up, then, denying women access to particular registers of language (written and learned language) by denying them the necessary education and persuading them they do not need/merit it affects both their state of knowledge and their state of consciousness. Even where male-controlled registers later become available to women, women may be negatively defined in relation to them, especially if the registers in question are prestigious, and negative attitudes may persist for a long time. (Thus no one now thinks it remarkable that Anglophone women can read and write, but it is still remarkable that they should write poetry or mathematical treatises.) The power of negative attitudes is something we must return to in our discussion of institutional and bureaucratic language.

INSTITUTIONAL LANGUAGE: COMMUNICATING IN URBAN SOCIETIES

If literacy is a problem for the underprivileged in less developed countries, bureaucracy is a major linguistic headache for the underprivileged of modern western cities. In two recent books advocating a new approach to communication ('interactional sociolinguistics')[22] the linguist John Gumperz points out how important 'communicative skills' have become with the growth of state and other bureaucracies (health, education, employment and tax services, for instance) in modern industrial society. More and more frequently, individuals in their everyday lives are having to negotiate linguistic interactions with these bureaucracies, and the result is that

> The ability to manage or adapt to diverse communicative situations has become essential and the ability to interact with people with whom one has no personal acquaintance is crucial to acquiring even a small measure of personal and social control. We have to talk in order to establish our rights and entitlements.... Communicational resources thus form an integral part of an individual's symbolic and social capital.[23]

The individual needs to be able to interact effectively with institutions and their representatives. Since it is the individual, for the most part, who wants something from the encounter, 'effectively' will mean 'in conformity with the norms of the institution'. Those who cannot express themselves in a way the bureaucracy finds acceptable (or minimally, comprehensible) will be disadvantaged.

Gumperz and his associates have produced a good deal of work on 'crosstalk' or, in plain language, *misunderstanding* between individuals whose norms of interaction are different. Their work has focused mainly on interactions between bureaucrats of various kinds (social workers, clerks, personnel managers) and Asian speakers of English, but the two main points that emerge from it are equally applicable to other ethnic minorities, working-class speakers in certain situations and, of course, women talking to men.

The first point is simply that socially distant individuals (especially those differentiated by ethnicity) do not share rather subtle strategies for structuring and interpreting talk, and this results in misunderstanding which can be frustrating for both parties and seriously disadvantageous for the Asian trying to get a job or a Social Security cheque. The second point, which is rather less explicit in Gumperz's books, is that bureaucracies use their experience of interethnic misunderstanding to generate representations of Asians as defective or inadequate communicators – representations which derive from racist stereotypes and reinforce racism. It is important to note that the right to represent and stereotype is not mutual, and that the power asymmetry here has serious consequences. Undoubtedly the Asians have their own less than complimentary ideas about the *gore* (white people), but these are the ideas of people without power. They do not serve as a base for administrative procedures and decisions, nor do they get expressed routinely in mass media: whereas institutional stereotypes of Asians *do* inform procedures, decisions and media representations. If Asians are defined as inadequate language users, they become *de facto* inadequate (crudely, no one listens any more to what they are actually saying, simply filtering it through the negative stereotype) and as Gumperz points out, in a modern industrial society this can have disastrous consequences.

It is important for feminists to ask whether women have the same ability as men to interact with people 'with whom one has no personal acquaintance' and 'adapt to diverse communicational situations'. If not, why not? Are women routinely misunderstood by men who have power over them, with disadvantageous results? Do men represent women as inadequate communicators, thus reducing their precious 'symbolic and social capital'? The question of misunderstanding between women and men has been addressed by two of Gumperz's associates, Daniel

Maltz and Ruth Borker, and they believe that the subcultural differences between Asian and white speakers are paralleled by
male/female differences.[24] Using the available literature on
children's talk and play patterns they argue that females and
males in western culture do in fact form separate subcultures,
and that this significantly affects male/female interaction.
Women and men do not attempt to do the same things in the
same way when they talk, and thus there is likely to be a rather
poor fit between what the speaker intends and what an opposite-
sex hearer picks up.

It seems likely that there is a good deal in this idea, though
Maltz and Borker do depend heavily on the competition versus
co-operation stereotype which I have already criticised (Chapter
3) and which is itself inspired by a lot of rather dubious literature.
My main reservation is that the sociolinguistic analysis of subcultural differences ought to include far more discussion about
the political structure superimposed on these differences. In other
words, Maltz and Borker say very little about the power of male
definitions of female speakers, the use of such definitions to
exclude women from certain registers and devalue their contribution to others. This omission is what I shall try to make good in
the remainder of the chapter.

DISCOURSES AND REGISTERS

I have already discussed the exclusion of women from written and
learned 'registers' (i.e. kinds of language appropriate in content,
style and tone to a particular domain of use, say 'scholarship' or
'legal documents' or 'religion') and pointed out that whereas it
makes no sense at all to speak of women not possessing 'language'
it is quite in order to say that, for historically specific reasons,
they may be forbidden to use certain registers at particular times
and in particular places. Registers of language historically
created by men very often represent women as marginal or
inferior, and may well continue to do so even after women have
begun to use them (in this book we have already looked at the
registers of news reporting and lexicography, and while these
practices were undoubtedly masculine originally, they have long
been open to women without any noticeable diminution in their

sexism). Partly this conservatism reflects the importance of tradition, 'custom and practice' in institutions. The conventions codified in style-books, rule-books, standing orders, editing and sub-editing manuals are quite literally handed down from generation to generation of professionals. They are part of a professional mystique, sanctified by history and enforced very often by the authoritarian training and advancement procedures of hierarchical organisations (the Civil Service and political parties, for instance). Partly, however, it reflects more general ideological matters. This point has been made very forcefully by semiologists like Roland Barthes (whose work on the ideological determinants of literary style in France remains a classic demonstration), Michel Foucault, Michel Pêcheux, Colin McCabe, Maria Black and Rosalind Coward.

Semiologists refer to what I have been calling 'registers' as *discourses* (McCabe representatively defines a discourse as a set of statements formulated on 'particular institutional sites of language use').[25] Each discourse needs to be understood in relation to its own conventions (thus TV chat shows and court cases exemplify different linguistic norms) and its functions in society.

Maria Black and Rosalind Coward, in the article on Dale Spender I have already discussed, explicitly say that discourse and not language (by which they mean *langue*) is the proper place for feminists to concentrate their efforts.

> Linguistic systems . . . serve as the basis for the production and interpretation of related utterances – discourses – which effect and sustain the different categorizations and positions of women and men. It is on these discourses and not on language in general or linguistic systems, that feminist analyses have to focus.[26]

By concentrating on discursive regularities (for instance, the use of generic masculine pronouns or the linguistic representation of women in the reporting of rape trials) we will discover more about the relation between language use and patriarchal ideology to which not only men but a great many women also subscribe.

What is stressed both in the semiologists' approach and in my own register-based approach is the *materiality* of the practices in question. Thus rather than posit, as Dale Spender does, a historically ubiquitous and unobservable operation by which males regulate meaning through an underlying semantic rule pejorating words for women, linguistic materialists look for the historical moment and circumstances in which a particular practice arose and the specific group who initiated it or whose authority and interests maintain it. We rarely find that a practice is initiated/maintained by all men (an exception might be the practice of pornoglossic intimidation discussed in Chapter 4) or that it extends into every linguistic register. The negative relation of women not to 'language' or 'meaning' but to various discourses is a variable and piecemeal affair.

Nevertheless, it seems to me that ultimately this piecemeal linguistic disadvantage must be related to the general roles and representations of women in their various cultures. Not every area of language use is regulated by obvious and consciously invoked conventions, and we must now turn to the part played be folklinguistic value judgements and gender-role expectations in silencing women and representing their speech as inadequate. We must consider in particular the Dalston Study Group's assertion that women's day-to-day language is undervalued even by women themselves, and that the disadvantaged 'doubt the strength and potential of their own language'. Is women's language in fact strong and full of potential, or is it repressed/suppressed, impoverished and inauthentic? How could women be persuaded to suppress or undervalue their own speech? To answer these questions we will need to look at the creation and regulation of femininity itself.

SILENCE: A WOMAN'S GLORY?

Some very obviously male-dominated metalinguistic practices are the customs and traditions of public speaking, which normally require women to be silent in public gatherings and on formal occasions. The key to this cross-culturally widespread phenomenon is, as Jenkins and Kramarae observe, the boundary between the private or familial, and the public or rhetorical. 'We find that women's sphere includes the interpersonal but seldom the rhetorical.'[27] In many societies different linguistic registers, dialects or even languages are used to mark the private/rhetorical boundary. And it is part of women's role generally, not just linguistically, to symbolise the private as opposed to the public. When this split is important in organising a society (as in most capitalist societies) women are important in defining the boundaries of the private.

An illustration of female marginality in the public and ritual speech of our own culture is provided by the etiquette of the wedding reception. Here we have a number of visible roles distributed between males and females equally: bride and groom, mothers and fathers, bridesmaids and best man, etc. Yet the women are ritually silent. The bride's father proposes a toast to the happy couple; the groom replies, proposing a toast to the bridesmaids which is replied to by the best man. Men speak, women are spoken for: here we have an epitome of women's position as 'seen and not heard'.

Is this the same as children being 'seen and not heard?' Cora Kaplan, in her essay 'Language and Gender', argues that it is.[28] Children are subject to restrictions on their speech in adult company, but whereas boys are eventually admitted to public speaking rights (Kaplan fixes this at puberty, the onset of adulthood and symbolically the beginning of manhood) girls are never allowed to grow up in the same way. Their participation in political, literary, formal, ritual and public discourse is not tolerated in the same way that children's participation is not. This view seems to me to be open to a number of objections, the main one being that restrictions on women speaking are often far stricter than those affecting children, and appear to be linked with explicitly *sexual* rites of passage. I am thinking here of the many taboos on women's speech discussed by Ardener and Smith.[29] It is not uncommon to find women being forbidden to speak for a set period after marriage, or to find men censuring the conduct of married women who allow their voices to be heard outside the private house.[30] Books of etiquette and advice to brides also warn that a married women must underline her wifely deference with wifely silence. In other words, silence is part of femininity, rather than being an absence of male privilege.

UNACCUSTOMED AS I AM...

Women as public speakers suffer not only from the customs that

silence them, but also from negative value-judgements on their
ability to speak effectively at all. Whatever style a culture deems
appropriate to the public arena, women are said to be less skilled
at using; whatever style is considered natural in women is deemed
unsuitable for rhetorical use. So, for example, Jespersen thinks
indirectness typical of women's style, mentioning 'their instinctive
shrinking from coarse and gross expressions and their preference
for refined and . . . veiled and indirect expressions'.[31] This lack of
'vigour and vividness' is what makes women unfit to be great
orators. Among the Malagasy, however, things are rather
different. Here the favoured style for ritual speech or *Kabary* is
indirect and allusive. Women's speech is thought to be direct and
vigorous, and thus women are once again debarred from public
speaking.[32]

It is necessary, as always, to treat the interaction between
actual usage and folklinguistic stereotype with the utmost care.
The excessively ladylike style 'described' by Jespersen is unlikely
ever to have been used consistently by women: it is the usual
idealisation based on the usual mixture of prejudice and wishful
thinking. But folklinguistic beliefs are never without significance,
and certainly this kind of belief, expressed in a score of passages
masquerading as description in anti-feminist tracts, etiquette
books, grammars and even feminist writings, have an effect on
how women think they speak and how they think they ought to
speak. In formal situations where speech is monitored closely,
women may indeed converge toward the norms of the mythology,
obeying the traditional feminine commandments (silence, not
interrupting, not swearing and not telling jokes).

VALUE

Folklinguistics inculcates an important set of value judgements on
the speech and writing of the two sexes. A whole vocabulary exists
denigrating the talk of women who do not conform to male ideas
of femininity: nag, bitch, strident. More terms trivialise interaction between women: girls' talk, gossip, chitchat, mothers'
meeting. This double standard of judgement is by no means
peculiar to linguistic matters. It follows the general rule that 'if in
anti-feminist discourse women are often inferior to men, nothing
in this same discourse is more ridiculous than a woman who

imitates a male activity and is therefore no longer a woman'.[33] This can apply not only to speaking or writing, but also to the way a woman looks, the job she does, the way she behaves sexually, the leisure pursuits she engages in, the intellectual activities she prefers and so on *ad infinitum*. Sex differentiation must be rigidly upheld by whatever means are available, for men can be men only if women are unambiguously women.

This imperative leads to an attitude toward the upbringing of women summed up in 1762 by Jean-Jacques Rousseau:

> In order for [women] to have what they need . . . we must give it to them, we must want to give it to them, we must consider them deserving of it. They are dependent on our feelings, on the price we put on their merits, on the value we set on their attractions and on their virtues. . . . Thus women's entire education should be planned in relation to men. To please men, to be useful to them, to win their love and respect, to raise them as children, care for them as adults, counsel and console them, make their lives sweet and pleasant: these are women's duties in all ages and these are what they should be taught from childhood on.[34]

In this notorious passage Rousseau gives us an account of why this sort of femininity must be constructed (to make men's lives 'sweet and pleasant'), how it is constructed (by indoctrination from childhood) and why women conform (because they are entirely dependent on men for the things they need).

Language, like every other aspect of female behaviour, has to be produced and regulated with this male-defined femininity in mind. Parental strictures, classroom practices and so on are designed to make the girl aware of her responsibility, and failure to conform may be punished with ridicule, loss of affection, economic and physical hardship. In short, then, we must treat the restrictions on women's language as part of a more general restricted feminine role. We cannot understand women's relation to language or to any other cultural phenomenon, unless we examine how in different societies those with power have tailored customs and institutions so they fit Rousseau's analysis and obey his prescription.

THE LIMITS OF CONTROL

This model of male dominance locates the linguistic mechanisms of control both in explicit rules and well-known customs restricting women's speech, and in the 'voluntary' constraints women place on themselves to be feminine, mindful of the real disadvantages attendant on failure. Since these mechanisms are not located in immutable mental or unconscious structures, control can only be partial, and even women's silence has its limits.

The more radical feminist theorists have often been unduly pessimistic because they did not acknowledge the limits of control and silence. When Dale Spender claims,

> One simple...means of curtailing the dangerous talk of women is to restrict their opportunities for talk....Tradition-ally, for women there have been no comparable locations to the pub which can encourage woman talk; there have been no opportunities for talk like those provided by football or the union meeting. Because women have been without the space and the place to talk they have been deprived of access to discourse *with each other*.[35]

she is simply wrong. If Spender is thinking here of the 'captive wife' alone with small children in an isolated flat, this is a relatively recent and restricted phenomenon. Even in middle-class Anglophone culture women's talk with each other is an important part of social organisation:[36] in other cultures, where segregation is often the norm both occupationally and socially, women's lives revolve around interaction with each other.

Spender is trying to make a case for the subversive nature of women's talk with each other, but by ignoring the age-old oral culture of women (as she must, to argue this case convincingly) she misleads us into accepting what is only a half-truth. Women's talk is not subversive per se: it becomes subversive when women begin to attach importance to it and to privilege it over their interactions with men (as in the case of consciousness-raising). Men trivialise the talk of women not because they are afraid of any such talk, but in order to make women themselves downgrade it. If women feel that all interaction with other women is a poor substitute for mixed interaction, and trivial compared with the profundities of men's talk, their conversations will indeed be harmless.

WOMEN'S TALK: THE MYTH OF IMPOVERISHMENT

Recently, feminists have begun to research women's talk. The picture that emerges from their studies is not one of silent or inarticulate women who struggle to express their experiences and feelings. On the contrary, it is of a rich verbal culture.[37] Moreover, that culture has a long history (if obscure: male metalinguistic practices strike again, this time by omission). It may be appropriate to see early women poets breaking through silence and absence, working in a genre where they were insecure and had no rights, but the ordinary woman speaker in her peer group cannot be adequately treated in this way.

To sociolinguists this story will have a familiar ring to it. One of the most celebrated achievements of sociolinguistics in the 1960s and early 1970s was to put working-class black American speech on the map through painstaking study of the vernacular black speakers used amongst themselves. Before the sociolinguist Labov and his associates undertook this research, using a methodology specifically designed to win the informants' co-operation (see Chapter 3), conventional wisdom among commentators on black language was that its speakers developed silent and inarticulate because they grew up in a linguistically deprived culture, were seldom addressed by their parents and not encouraged to speak themselves. The dialect they came to school speaking was labelled 'a basically non-logical form of expressive behaviour' or, in the terms of Bernstein a *restricted code*.[38]

Bernstein's code theory (which was developed with the English class structure, rather than American ethnic differences, in mind) holds that the two types of socialisation typical of the middle and working classes respectively, give rise to differing relations to language. The middle-class child controls both a restricted code (roughly emotional, illogical, inexplicit and incorrect, useful for expressing group solidarity and feeling) and an elaborated code (which facilitates higher cognitive operations through its logic and explicitness). The working-class child controls only restricted code, and thus her ability to perform the sort of intellectual tasks expected at school is limited.

The claim that black children were restricted code only speakers, therefore, was an attempt to explain why they failed, or underachieved relative to white children, at school. It led to a compensatory education project in which children were taught the appropriate elaborated code (i.e. white middle-class English). The sociolinguist Labov showed that this project, and the premises underlying it, were fundamentally misguided.[39] For one thing, the linguistic features defining elaborated code turned out to be nothing more than an amalgam of middle-class habits (like use of the passive and the pronoun *one*): it was hard to argue they had any inherent value. The features stigmatised in black English were not failed attempts at standard English, but systematic variations, or more accurately, parts of a related but different dialect. In other words, it was (and is) fundamentally unclear whether there is such a thing as a restricted code which is unable to express complex ideas, logical relationships and so on.

In the second place, Labov demonstrated that black children grow up in an extremely stimulating verbal culture with its own rituals. Individuals who at school were silent or inarticulate were very likely to metamorphose, within their peer group, into skilled verbal performers. To unearth the rich verbal culture of black adolescents, Labov had to go to a great deal of trouble, for they did not willingly display it to white outsiders – which was why successive experiments had failed to elicit anything but silence and inarticulacy. Labov used a young black fieldworker to elicit a wide range of data, and in analysing it he deliberately abandoned his educated middle-class notions of correctness and formality. Labov concluded that black children failed in school mainly because they had no motivation to succeed. They defined themselves in opposition to dominant white values, and to be fully integrated members of their peer group they had to express disdain for formal education.

Other studies of nonstandard language users (to use the term *restricted code* would be to beg the question linguistically, as I have already pointed out) stress that there is a linguistic problem, but not in the language itself so much as in the stigma people attach to it. In other words, the theory of codes could be boiled down to an essentially political truism: those who do not speak the language of the dominant elite will find it difficult to get on.

I have dealt with Bernstein's code theory in detail because I think there are parallels in it with the case of women, and that feminists could learn a number of lessons from the controversy it provoked.

Women are not in quite the same position as working-class and black speakers. Their language is less obviously different from men's than working-class from middle-class or black from white varieties, and the differences are much more often below the level of speakers' consciousness. Nor has anyone yet suggested that women's speech variety is responsible for massive educational under-achievement. In many respects, however, women's language has been treated as if it were a type of restricted code. And this evaluation has come both from feminists (who speak of the silence and inarticulacy of women and their culture, and of the inauthenticity with which they have been forced to express themselves) and by old fashioned gallants and chauvinists. Jespersen, for instance, presents the features which typify female speech as products of an impoverished cognitive apparatus whose shortcomings are surprisingly similar to those detailed by Bernstein in his descriptions of restricted-code speakers. Even the linguistic hallmarks of restricted code and women's language are the same: a preference for conjoining over the more complex embedding, unfinished sentences, and a heavy reliance on intonation rather than more 'explicit' syntactic devices.[40] Writers agree, in short, that there are various things women's language is inadequate to express.

Except in so far as it applies to all communication, this strikes me as a false and dangerous belief. Perhaps research now being done on women in small groups, on female folklore and culture, will break it down, both by showing that women have rich and complex verbal resources, and by proving that the folklinguistic consensus on women's speech style is inaccurate. Researchers in this latter area should focus, as I have tried to do in this book, on the connections and similarities between feminist and anti-feminist folklinguistic beliefs, and on the importance of value judgements in producing what disadvantage women do suffer as speakers and writers.

It is also important to make explicitly the connection between *women* as disadvantaged speakers and the disadvantaging of other subordinate groups such as ethnic minorities and the working class. Such groups could certainly learn from the WLM's refusal to ignore questions of language and politics; on the other hand, the WLM in making those links might be moved to revalue certain theoretical excesses.

As the Dalston Study group observe, 'Immigrants and working-class people too have a negative point of entry into our culture, something no one has yet explained with reference to the penis/phallus.'[41] If language is an important political and personal resource, feminism cannot afford a theory that tells women only how they are oppressed as speakers: it must convince them also of 'the strength and potential of their own language'.

Although the nature of communication is such that men cannot appropriate meaning nor completely control women's use of language, they (or a subset of them) control important institutions and practices. The effect of that control is to give men certain rights over women and to hedge women around with restrictions and myths. Its mechanisms range from explicit rules against women speaking in public or on ritual occasions to folk-linguistic beliefs and values denigrating women's language and obscuring female verbal culture. These rules, prescriptions and beliefs can be related on the one hand to femininity in general, and on the other, to the linguistic and cultural subordination of other oppressed groups.

Whereas the current feminist belief in determinism, male control and female alienation offers very little prospect of struggle and liberation, we get a more hopeful picture when we concentrate on metalinguistic and discursive processes linked to women's identity and role in particular societies. These processes can be challenged much more easily and effectively than *langue*, meaning, alienation and other such abstractions. Practice and strategy are one subject to be taken up in the conclusion.

WL

9 Conclusion: Feminism and Linguistic Theory: Problems and Practices

> If one continues to believe in the
> project of human speech, one must
> move beyond a view of language as
> simply or inexorably 'power over',
> discourse as domination...and toward
> speech as part of an emancipatory
> effort, a movement toward social
> clarity and self-comprehension.
>
> *Jean Bethke Elshtain*

At the beginning of this book I set out to assess the state of the art with regard to language in feminist theory. In this conclusion we must draw all the threads together, pinpoint the outstanding problems and − most important − examine the implications for a radical linguistic practice.

In the course of my discussion I have dealt with a diverse group of theorists addressing themselves to a wide range of questions from a large number of political, linguistic and philosophical perspectives. So in drawing the threads together the first problem must be this: can we assemble all these viewpoints into one coherent theoretical framework, and is it desirable to do so? Undoubtedly, there are many who find the diversity of approaches in this field problematic. Faced with writers who experiment with frameworks from all over the social sciences (Kramarae[1]) or cobble together an eclectic approach (Spender[2]), reviewers of the literature have occasionally bemoaned the lack of any theoretical pigeonhole to put questions of language and sex in. One recent reviewer, by insisting that 'We need a coherent theory within which work can be done on the subject of the inter-action between sexual gender...and language,[3] implicitly acknowledges that we haven't currently got one, and that this is a bad thing. Feminists may choose to regard this as a non-problem, either because they scoff at all theory, or, more likely, because they reject the implied criticism of borrowers and cobblers as pointless purism. Many may feel, in addition, that pluralism is healthy and stimulating, whereas orthodoxy would be depressing.

Nevertheless, it could be argued that the present state of affairs is not so much pluralistic as simply confused. For even if we can never come up with a synthesis of all our viewpoints and frameworks (and this looks more than likely, given the tensions between reformism and radicalism, or empiricism and subject-theory) it should be possible in a pluralist world to initiate dialogue between theorists who disagree: and as things stand this is a far from straightforward enterprise. The areas of disagreement are still insufficiently clear, and theorists still either unable or reluctant to spell out what issues are at stake.

A feminist linguistic theory, in my opinion, is a theory that links language with sex in two ways: it spells out the connection on the one hand between language and gender identity, and on the other hand between language and women's oppression. If we are to have useful dialogue, therefore, all feminist linguistic theories must make it clear where they stand on four basic questions. First, what are we talking about when we talk about language? Secondly, what do we mean by *women's language* (or indeed *men's language*): how is the link between language and gender to be understood? Thirdly, what is the relation of language to reality? Fourthly, what is the relation of language to disadvantage, particularly (but not exclusively) in the case of women?

Definite answers to these four questions would provide a basis both for fruitful debate amongst differing theoretical tendencies, and for the development of a feminist practice in speech and writing. The remainder of the conclusion will therefore be devoted to examining the questions in more detail, focusing especially on the problems that are not satisfactorily resolved by the theories I have surveyed so far.

WHAT ARE WE TALKING ABOUT WHEN WE TALK ABOUT LANGUAGE?

One of the most difficult terms to grasp in feminist writing about language is the deceptively simple word *language* itself, since this word is often used with a generality bordering on the vacuous. For instance, a feminist writes that women are oppressed by language; but the next sentence makes it clear she is speaking of art and mythology.[4] There is no apparent distinction between literal and metaphorical uses of the term.

Similarly, we can read in feminist writing of 'the grammar of moral discourse' and 'the language of theory'.[5] But what are we talking about? Does 'the language of theory,' for instance, mean 'the sort of words used in theories' or 'the type of syntax used in theoretical writings' or just 'what is said in theories'? Are women excluded from theoretical language because the lexical definitions of theory writers excluded our perspective, because the syntax customary in theory writing is alien to our way of dealing with ideas, because we disagree with what theories assert, or because our participation in theoretical discourse would be considered unfeminine? And are all these possibilities equally matters of *language*?

Because it is usually impossible to tell, there is a tendency to take these phrases on trust, to skip over them and accept whatever proposition rests upon their use. Yet the implications and possible lines of attack are very different depending on whether we are talking about words, syntax, content or custom. In other words, unless we formulate our critique of language with a certain linguistic precision, our theory will not tell us how to proceed in practice with our struggle. Instead of demystifying patriarchal language, we have produced an analysis which, if it achieves anything, achieves only further mystification.

This is not to say that a theory of language must exclude art, or myth, or the metalinguistic customs that regulate language use. What matters is simply that we should all know what we are talking about. Theory making is the paradigm example of an activity in which our metalinguistic skill for defining terms is relevant, and even vital. We cannot leave the definition of *language* to the vagaries of context as we would in ordinary conversation, because we are trying for something less hit-and-miss than the cross-purpose talk of an ordinary interchange.

It also seems likely that problems of definition have a real bearing on apparently more intractable problems of theory. For instance, it might be argued that the language-and-reality problem arises very largely out of an over-wide interpretation of the word *language*. Because we use language to learn about and reflect on other social phenomena, the story goes, all those social phenomena must in the end reduce to language. The minute we start to consider what we mean by *language* this assertion looks less secure. Examining definitions leads to a healthy questioning of assumptions.

Another crucial distinction blurred in the term *language* is the difference between speech and writing. Linguists have a dogma on this subject to go along with their dogmas on prescriptivism and objectivity: they say that speech is more basic than writing, and writing is no more than a graphic representation of speech. But the reality of linguistic practice, and indeed of people's language-use, is entirely different.

In practice, linguists treat speech as though it were a poor imitation of writing. You can see this in the fact that linguistics has long taken the complete sentence as its standard unit of analysis, even though most spontaneous speech contains rather few complete sentences. Thus complicated 'editing rules' have to be posited to account for the divergence of speech from the ideal and much of what the linguist hears is defined as 'ungram-matical'. Prosodic features like stress, rhythm and intonation are marginalised. All this points to the existence of writing as a hidden norm rather than a second-order representation (indeed, the claim that writing is just transcribed speech is falsified the minute the two are actually compared). Yet many of the claims made for and against the language of women by semiologists and linguists alike rest on the same prejudice that speech is 'really' just writing in a different form. Consider Kristeva's placing of the prosodic, that is to say, rhythm, stress and intonation, in the semiotic order while logical syntax goes in the symbolic order. For speech this is a wholly artificial separation. Syntactic functions are carried out to a very great extent by prosodic devices when we talk, and writing is arguably much impoverished by the fact that it cannot combine the affective and the logical in the same way. One could only ever marginalise the prosodic as something extra rather than integral to communication if one took writing, not speech, as the norm of language use. Once that is admitted, claims that women use intonation rather than grammar can be revealed for what they are: meaningless. A similar fate must also befall Luce Irigaray's claim that feminine language has nothing to do with the syntax of the complete sentence. Unless she makes it clear she is talking of feminine *writing*, the obvious retort is that no one's language has much to do with the syntax of the complete sentence. The complete sentence is entirely an artefact of literacy.

When we consider the demands put forward for a feminine 'language', however, it is very soon clear that the feminists concerned *are* thinking only of writing. For the kind of feminine language they envisage is literally unspeakable, however writeable it may be. It has puns made in the spelling, the punctuation and through diacritic makings; the structure is convoluted, needing considerable time to produce and to process. Snatches of unconnected discourses may be juxtaposed in a way that requires careful reading. Even the less formally difficult strategies, such as Mary Daly's constant parenthetical interrogation of etymology and structure in the words she uses, would be either tedious or just impossible in talk.

Of course, textual strategies need not be rejected just because they won't do for speech. On the contrary, the medium of the written word should be exploited for all it's worth. But isn't it a sort of cheating, nevertheless, to talk of language and mean only written language? To generalise about language (as Kristeva and Irigaray do) in terms that do not apply to the vast majority of language users and language events? Unfortunately, this criticism is as true of linguistics as it is of Kristevan semiology. 'Scriptism' – a prejudice against speech as compared to writing – is ingrained in the western tradition and constitutes one of the most serious misunderstandings of the nature of human communication so far embranced even by linguistic science. Any radical theory of language must be on its guard against scriptist tendencies and the many inaccuracies they engender.

LANGUAGE AND GENDER: MAKING THE CONNECTIONS

Once we have got clear what phenomena are to count as 'language' in our theory, we can go on to examine what we mean by 'women's language' and how people's use of language signals or interacts with or partly constitutes their identity as feminine or masculine. In fact every theorist has some notion of the framework in which women's identity and position is to be related to language, whether this is made explicit or not: by deliberately making explicit the frameworks used by the various writers we have looked at, we can isolate three main strands.

1 Subculture and gender role

Within the first approach, the important idea is of women and men forming separate subcultures. The differing speech of the two sexes is thus seen as a function of their differing roles; it derives from, and expresses, a whole complex of factors associated with social maleness/femaleness, including particular personality traits (e.g. in our own culture, masculine aggression and feminine passivity) and identity markers which derive from the sexual division of labour. Adherents of this point of view include the Ardeners, Maltz and Borker, Smith and the later Cheris Kramarae.

2 Dominance hierarchies

The second approach focuses on one particular aspect of the female role: its powerlessness relative to the male role. Women's speech therefore expresses no complex or specifically female role identity, but simply a low position in the social hierarchy. Women use an inherently powerless style of speech, but it is not peculiar to their sex; it may be used by anyone in a position of relative powerlessness. Haden-Elgin representatively asserts, 'There is no such thing as a specific 'women's language'. . . . Rather there are dominant and subordinate language modes, and women, being a subordinate group, are frequently found using these subordinate modes.'[6] Robin Lakoff also belongs to the 'dominance hierarchy' camp, holding that women's language has nothing to do with femininity per se, and everything to do with women's subordinate status.

3 Sexuality and the body

Finally, we have seen that there are many theorists who believe that language is related to gender identity through its intimate connection with the body and sexual desire. Adherents of this view (most strongly endorsed by Hélène Cixous and Luce Irigaray) usually argue that the feminine language of which they speak does not yet exist: it is a utopian goal rather than a describable reality.

These three contrasting explanations of the link between language and gender imply very different political practices. If the link is gender role (a complex of personality and occupational traits, socially conditioned values and beliefs regarding sexual differentiation) then it would be feasible for us to revalue feminine styles of speech. We could make our language into a badge of our identity as women who are proud to be women. If on the other hand the link is nothing more than relative power, it is incumbent upon us to jettison our powerless way of talking as something that reinforces our powerless position in a vicious circle. We should all take assertiveness training and start talking like men. Or if the link really is sexuality and the rhythms of the female body, we must reject all current models of speech and strive towards a discourse that doesn't yet exist. In many ways, these three alternatives correspond to Kristeva's three feminisms: Lakoff represents liberal feminism (make women and men equal), Kramarae represents radical feminism (revalue the distinctively feminine) and Cixous is the revolutionary (refuse existing classifications).

For most feminists, the notion of a language close to the body and sexual desire is still problematic, either an impossibility or something to be found only in the 'heightened' language of poetry. The question of power versus role is more acute, however, For while it clearly will not do to say that women are nothing but passive victims, that their cultural products express nothing more complicated than sheer powerlessness, or that their language is just like the language of all other oppressed groups, on the other hand it will not do to formulate any kind of female identity that takes no account of the reality of powerlessness. Powerlessness is an important factor in women's lives and in the identities they forge. Theoretically, then, the choice between 'dominance' and 'subculture' theories is a false choice, and similarly the practical choice between rejection and revaluation is not clear-cut. In conclusion, then, we need a more complex way of linking ways of speaking and writing to our multifaceted identities as women.

LANGUAGE AND REALITY

We have already seen that the issue of language and reality – of linguistic determinism – is central to the dispute between theoretical reformists and radicals. However, the issue itself remains unresolved, and this requires discussion. Most theories take up an absolute position on the question of language and reality. Either they see language quite unproblematically as a reflection of something else – usually an ill-defined 'social organisation' or 'thought' – or else they see it, equally unproblematically, as the source of that mental or social reality. Moreover, the terms of the debate are set in such a way that there cannot be any answer in between the two extremes. Opponents of determinism appeal to notions of common sense and to free-will, which they accuse the radicals of denying: determinists, on the other hand, accuse non-believers of naviety and of clinging to an essentialist conception of human nature and experience which is inaccurate, outmoded and irrevocably bourgeois. But is there really nothing in between? Can there be a theory that is neither essentialist nor determinist in the radical sense?

I do not believe that language is the first cause, and I see nothing wrong with asserting that meaning derives from something we might call experience, as well as from immediate context. However, that does not mean I believe in some central core of human nature (though I might posit a core of human cognitive abilities/rationality, given by the nature of our bodies and brains) nor in the existence of an inner mental world untouched by social forces. There is no pre-existent and innocent subjectivity on which a layer of ideology is somehow to be superimposed. On the contrary I agree with the semiologists and with all anti-humanists that our 'personalities', our desires, our needs, our ways of behaving, are constructed in our interactions with the world. These constructed elements are our real selves, and not just some kind of false consciousness that can simply be stripped away. I accept, also, that we are complex creatures who cannot fully understand our own actions, influenced as they are by factors of which we remain wholly unconscious.

What I cannot accept, however, is the privileged status accorded language in this process of construction. Of course it plays some part – it cannot be just a reflection of other things, for it is basic to much of our experience – but other things are important too: perhaps even more important, for they happen earlier in our lives and are less able than language to become objects of reflection and interpretation in their own right. I am thinking of socio-familial relations; of the division of labour and economic organisation that regulates societies; of the physical environment; of individual genetic make-up. All these things interact with each other and with the situations we happen to be in to produce what I would call experience, a body of relationships and interactions with the world that inform behaviour in complex ways. The acquisition and interpretation of this experience is a never-ending process.

Those who seek to understand the workings of human societies must resist the temptation to reduce them to a single generating principle. Relations of production, relations with parents and siblings, language – it is always simplistic to set up one variable as basic. The quest for a first cause is like asking which came first, the chicken or the egg. Luckily, it is still possible to ask how chickens produce eggs, and how eggs produce chickens, even if the question of which came first remains for ever unanswered. The either/or debate in feminist linguistic theory is equally fruitless; and what is really needed is a radical questioning on both sides of their taken-for-granted notions about the production of meaning.

LANGUAGE AND DISADVANTAGE

The premise of any feminist linguistic theory must be that language and oppression, language and disadvantage, are somehow connected. That language is a resource of the powerful (or at least, that it can be used thus) and a potential instrument of oppression is not in doubt.

But one tendency it seems to me we must counter as much as possible is the extraordinary tendency, illustrated throughout this book, to blame what happens to people on the sort of language they use. This has been a popular explanation for some time: working-class and black children under-achieve at school because their language is inadequate, communism triumphs because the

Russian language has been corrupted, women are marginal and negative social beings because their language is ineffectual/ inauthentic. Linguistic reform is the key to all that is good, there- fore, from equality of opportunity to democracy and Truth.

But how could language per se be responsible for disadvant- age? Certainly it would be easy and convenient to believe it was: under-achieving children could be given 'compensatory' education, women could do assertiveness training, Asians could be taught code-switching and the Russian dictionary could be written by the United Nations. No one in a privileged position need change, or give up, anything. We need not ask questions about our standards of adequate and inadequate language use, nor consider where they came from in the first place. And above all, we need not admit that the institutions of society dis- advantage the poor, the black and the female just because they are poor, or black, or female. We can go on pretending that language change (or education, or equal opportunity laws) is enough. It seems to me that this is a particular pernicious lie which linguists have a responsibility to expose. The use of linguistic and metalinguistic resources to oppress others should not be ignored; but we must acknowledge the limitation of theories of oppression that do not go beyond the linguistic.

CHANGING OUR PRACTICE: TOWARD A RADICAL DISCOURSE

In this book I have reached the conclusion that no perfect feminist speech or writing style exists, nor could one ever exist. Moreover, the changes normally demanded by feminists have distinct disadvantages: the writing style sometimes held to be close to feminist ideals is also particularly difficult, so that it is open to charges of elitism, while the non-sexist language advocated by the reformist tendency has at its core a politically dangerous illusion, the illusion of sexual neutrality. Yet even if we believe that non-sexist language is little better than ordinary sexist language, the demand that people change their usage can be liberating. For one thing, it cannot fail to draw attention to the present masculist bias of conventional usage; but more important, it calls into question the common-sense transparency and fixedness of meaning. The political importance of this has been ably discussed by Trevor Pateman. Pateman believes that people in our society are encouraged to engage in what he calls 'idle discourse'. Idle discourse dodges meaning, and, rather like the young Simone de Beauvoir, treats definitions as closed, not possible subjects for rational dispute. In other words, it is a meta-linguistically impoverished language in which meanings are static and taken for granted.

The existence of idle discourse is not a reflection of the nature of language. Discourse does not have to be idle, and its idleness is only a product of people's repressive socialisation and hopeless circumstances.

> 'Idle discourse is the language of the powerless who accept their position. To the degree that the pursuit of security dominates everyday thought and language use, I think this is because people have decided that other satisfactions are not obtainable.'[7]

Pateman appears to believe that what people do in their dealings with words they will do in other areas of their experience. The unthinking acceptance of other people's definitions will go hand-in-hand with a general reluctance to question the way the world operates. Anything that encourages people to reflect on language, and particularly on the provisional status of meaning and definition, is thus politically progressive. Pateman points out that outer changes, such as the use of non-sexist language, can affect inner attitudes ultimately, because they do as a matter of fact change the political status quo: 'the change in outward practice *constitutes* a restructuring of at least one aspect of one social relationship ... every act reproduces or subverts a social institution.'[8] This is an important point to make when some theorists are enquiring cynically what the difference is between macho men and those who have learned to say 'she'. The importance of linguistic change, and indeed of many other sorts of reform, is precisely that 'every act reproduces or subverts a social institution'. We always have a choice.

Pateman also points out that to make a change in the way you speak or write is to assume a certain responsibility for your relationship to the world and for your behaviour, in its way an act of the greatest political importance. 'For in my act I have asserted that I can control language; I have stopped acting as if language necessarily controls me.'[9] This is surely what Jean Bethke Elshtain means when she refers to speech as 'part of an emancipatory effort, a movement toward social clarity and self comprehension'. She goes on to add, 'the project of rational speech, an eyes-open, truth-telling passion against "the powers that be" and "the censors within" can be one emancipatory window into the future'.[10] Radical discourse, then, is the very opposite of idle discourse. It constantly questions the metalinguistic practices by which idle discourse is created and encouraged and thus by which power relationships are reproduced. It questions, also, the stability of meaning, and asserts very forcefully that we can change our usage by a conscious act of will.

Perhaps the most positive effect of changing our linguistic practice will be to destroy the pernicious belief that we have to be controlled and oppressed by our language. Once over that hurdle, we can start learning to speak out with confidence and to use the resources of language and metalanguage, so often denied us or used against us, in the continuing struggle against patriarchy.

NOTES

CHAPTER 1: INTRODUCTION

1. Philip M. Smith, 'Sex Markers in Speech', in K. Scherer and H. Giles (eds), *Social Markers in Speech* (CUP, 1979).
2. Casey Miller and Kate Swift, *The Handbook of Non-Sexist Writing* (Women's Press, 1980).
3. Betty Friedan, *The Feminine Mystique* (Gollancz, 1963).
4. Camilla Gugenheim, 'Man Made Language', *Amazon*, 4, 1981.
5. Mary Daly, *Gyn/Ecology: the Metaethics of Radical Feminism* (Women's Press, 1978).

CHAPTER 2: LINGUISTIC THEORY

1. E. Marks and I. de Courtivron (eds), *New French Feminisms* (Harvester Press, 1981).
2. F. de Saussure, *Course in General Linguistics*, trans. W. Baskin (Fontana, 1974) p. 16.
3. Ibid.
4. Roland Barthes, *Mythologies* (du Seuil, 1957).
5. Noam Chomsky, review of *Verbal Behavior, Language*, 35, 1959.
6. Dale Spender, *Man Made Language* (Routledge & Kegan Paul, 1980) and Cheris Kramarae, *Women and Men Speaking* (Newbury House, 1981).

CHAPTER 3: THE POLITICS OF VARIATION

1. Mercilee Jenkins and Cheris Kramarae, 'A Thief in the House: the Case of Women and Language', *Men's Studies Modified*, ed. Dale Spender (Pergamon, 1981).
2. Jonathan Swift, 'A Proposal for Correcting the English Tongue',

Prose Works of Jonathan Swift, vol. IV, ed. H. Davis (Blackwell, 1957).
3. O. Jespersen, *Language: Its Nature, Development and Origin* (Allen & Unwin, 1922).
4. Lecture on 'Varieties of English' given in Oxford by the Warden of Keble, 1982.
5. Robin Lakoff, *Language and Women's Place* (Harper & Row, 1975).
6. B. L. Dubois and I. Crouch, 'The Question of Tag-Questions in Women's Speech: They Don't Really Use More of Them, Do They?', *Language in Society*, 4, 1976.
7. D. Crystal and D. Davy, *Advanced Conversational English* (Longman, 1975).
8. H. P. Grice, 'Logic in Conversation', *Syntax and Semantics, III*, ed. P. Cole and J. L. Morgan (Academic Press, 1975).
9. Cheris Kramarae, *Women and Men Speaking* (Newbury House, 1981) p. 9.
10. R. F. Bales, 'How People Interact in Conferences', *Communication in Face to Face Interaction*, ed. J. Laver and S. Hutcheson (Penguin, 1972).
11. J. Pellowe, G. Nixon, B. Strang and V. McNeany, 'A Dynamic Modelling of Linguistic Variation: the Urban (Tyneside) Linguistic Survey', *Lingua*, 30, 1972.
12. Jenkins and Kramarae, op. cit., p. 16.
13. K. Scherer and H. Giles (eds), *Social Markers in Speech* (CUP, 1979).
14. Jenkins and Kramarae, op. cit., p. 16.
15. P. Trudgill, 'Sex, Covert Prestige and Linguistic Change in the Urban British English of Norwich', *Language in Society*, 1, 1972.
16. Elinor O. Keenan, 'Norm Makers, Norm Breakers; Uses of Speech by Women in a Malagasy Community', *Explorations in the Ethnography of Speaking*, ed. R. Bauman and J. Sherzer (CUP, 1974) p. 142.
17. Ibid., p. 141.
18. Christine Delphy, 'Women in Stratification Studies', *Doing Feminist Research*, ed. Helen Roberts, (Routledge & Kegan Paul, 1981).
19. Kramarae, op. cit.
20. D. Maltz and R. Borker, 'A Cultural Approach to Male/Female Miscommunication', *Language and Social Identity*, ed. J. Gumperz (CUP, 1982).
21. Lakoff, op. cit.
22. Caroline Henton, 'Sex Specific Phonetics and Social Realisation', unpublished 1983.

23. P. M. Smith, 'Sex Markers in Speech' *Social Markers in Speech*, ed. K. Scherer & H. Giles (CUP, 1979).
24. Dubois and Crouch, op. cit.
25. Dale Spender, *Man Made Language* (Routledge & Kegan Paul, 1980) p. 8.

CHAPTER 4: FALSE DICHOTOMIES

1. Simone de Beauvoir, *The Second Sex*, trans. Parshley (Vintage, 1974).
2. Luce Irigararay, *Ce Sexe qui n'en est pas un* (Minuit, 1977).
3. Jane Gallop, 'Psychoanalysis in France', *Women and Literature*, vol. 7, no 1, p. 61.
4. M. Bierwisch, 'Semantics', *New Horizons in Linguistics*, ed. J. Lyons (Penguin, 1970).
5. Dale Spender, *Man Made Language* (Routledge & Kegan Paul, 1980) p. 2.
6. Women's Journal.
7. Marielouise Janssen-Jurreit, *Sexism* (Pluto Press, 1982) p. 280.
8. John Lyons, *Introduction to Theoretical Linguistics* (CUP, 1968) p. 284.
9. Jakob Grimm, *Deutsche Grammatik*, quoted in Janssen-Jurreit, *Sexism: the Male Monopoly of History and Thought* (Pluto Press, 1982) p. 292.
10. Ibid., p. 297.
11. Anne Corbett, 'Cherchez la metaphor', *Guardian*, 18 Feb. 1983.
12. *Harvard Crimson*, quoted in C. Miller and K. Swift, *Words and Women* (Penguin, 1976) p. 92.
13. B. Dubois and I. Crouch, 'American Minority Women in Sociolinguistic Perspective' *IJSL*, 1978, p. 9.
14. Ann Bodine, 'Androcentrism in Prescriptive Grammar', *Language in Society*, 4, 1975.
15. Maria Black and Rosalind Coward, 'Linguistic, Social and Sexual Relations', *Screen Education*, 39, 1981.

CHAPTER 5: MAKING CHANGES

1. Stephen Kanfer, 'Sispeak', *Time*, 23 Oct. 1972.
2. C. Miller and K. Swift, *The Handbook of Non-Sexist Writing* (Women's Press, 1980).
3. C. Miller and K. Swift, *Words and Women: New Language in New Times* (Penguin, 1976).

4. Ibid., p. 8.
5. Muriel Schulz, 'The Semantic Derogation of Women', *Language and Sex: Difference and Dominance*, ed. B. Thorne and N. Henley (Newbury Hall, 1975).
6. Andrea Dworkin, *Pornography: Men Possessing Women* (Women's Press, 1981).
7. Mary Daly, *Gyn/Ecology: the Metaethics of Radical Feminism* (Women's Press, 1978).
8. Miller and Swift *Handbook*, p. 4.
9. Ibid., p. 8.
10. Cf. John Hall, *The Sociology of Literature* (Longman, 1979).
11. Miller and Swift, *Handbook*, p. 4.
12. I am indebted to Peter Mühlhäusler for pointing this out to me.
13. D. Mandelbaum (ed.), *Selected Writings of Edward Sapir* (University of California Press, 1949).
14. Roger Scruton, 'How Newspeak Leaves Us Naked', *The Times*, 2 Feb. 1983.

CHAPTER 6: SILENCE, ALIENATION AND OPPRESSION

1. Mary Daly, *Gyn/Ecology: the Metaethics of Radical Feminism* (Women's Press, 1978) p. 1.
2. Adrienne Rich, 'Power and Danger', in *On Lies, Secrets and Silence* (Virago, 1980) pp. 247–8.
3. F. de Saussure, *Course in General Linguistics*, trans. Baskin (Fontana, 1974) p. 112.
4. E. Marks and I. de Courtivron (eds), *New French Feminisms* (Harvester Press, 1981) p. xiii.
5. Ian Griffiths, 'Speech, Writing and Rewriting' (unpublished paper) p. 45.
6. Saussure, op. cit., p. 14.
7. D. Mandelbaum, *Selected Writings of Edward Sapir* (University of California Press, 1949) p. 162.
8. J. B. Carroll (ed.), *Language, Thought and Reality: Selected Writings of Benjamin Lee Whorf* (MIT Press 1976).
9. Mandelbaum, op. cit., p. 10.
10. Carroll op. cit., p. 253.
11. J. Lyons, *Introduction to Theoretical Linguistics* (CUP 1968) p. 434.
12. G. Orwell, 'Politics and the English Language', in *Selected Essays* (Secker & Warburg, 1961) p. 353.
13. Roger Scruton, 'How Newspeak Leaves Us Naked', *The Times*, 1 Feb. 1983.

14. Julia Kristeva, 'Woman Can Never Be Defined', interview with psych et po, in Marks and de Courtivron, op. cit., p. 140.
15. Marks and de Courtivron, op. cit., p. 3.
16. Shirley Ardener (ed.), *Perceiving Women* (Dent, 1975) p. xii.
17. Shirley Ardener, *Defining Females* (John Wiley, 1978) p. 21.
18. Edwin Ardener, 'Belief and the Problem of Women', in *Perceiving Women*, ed. S. Ardener, p. 22.
19. Ardener, *Defining Females*, p. 20.
20. Ibid., p. 21.
21. E. Ardener, op. cit.
22. Ardener, *Defining Females*, p. 20.
23. Ardener, *Perceiving Women*, p. ix.
23. Ibid., p. xxi.
24. Ardener, *Defining Females*, pp. 22–3.
25. Ibid.
26. D. Zimmerman and C. West, 'Sex Roles, Interruptions and Silences in Conversation', *Language and Sex: Difference and Dominance*, ed. B. Thorne and N. Henley (Newbury House, 1975).
27. Cheris Kramarae, *Women and Men Speaking* (Newbury House, 1981) p. 3.
28. Dale Spender, *Man Made Language* (Routledge & Kegan Paul, 1980) pp. 2–3.
29. Ibid., p. 3.
30. Ibid., p. 4.
31. Ibid., p. 139.
32. Ibid., p. 139.
33. D. Smith, 'A peculiar eclipsing: women's exclusion from men's culture', *WSIQ* 1, 1978, pp. 281–2.
34. Spender, op. cit., p. 1.

CHAPTER 7: SEMIOLOGY AND THE GENDERED SUBJECT

1. R. Coward and J. Ellis, *Language and Materialism* (Routledge & Kegan Paul, 1977), p. 153.
2. M. Black and R. Coward, 'Linguistic, Social and Sexual Relations', *Screen Education*, 39.
3. Cf. Christine Delphy, 'A Materialist Feminism is Possible', *Feminist Review*, 4.
4. Black and Coward, op. cit., p. 70.
5. Ibid., p. 72.
6. Ibid., p. 72.

7. Ibid., p. 81.
8. Toril Moi, 'Who's Afraid of Virginia Woolf: Feminist Readings of Woolf', 1982, p. 1.
9. Coward and Ellis, op. cit., p. 1.
10. F. de Saussure, *Course in General Linguistics*, trans. Baskin (Fontana, 1974) p. 14.
11. J. Mitchell and J. Rose (eds), *Feminine Sexuality* (Macmillan, 1982) p. 49.
12. Ibid., p. 42.
13. Coward and Ellis, op. cit., p. 97.
14. J. Lacan, *Le Seminaire XX: Encore* (Editions du Seuil, 1975) p. 68.
15. Toril Moi, op. cit., p. 14.
16. Toril Moi, 'Language, Femininity, Revolution: Julia Kristeva and Anglo-American Feminist Linguistics', unpublished lecture, 1983, p. 23.
17. L. Irigaray, 'Women's exile,' *Ideology and Consciousness*, 1, p. 62.
18. Ibid., p. 64.
19. Ibid., p. 65.
20. Ibid., p. 69.
21. Ibid., p. 71.
22. 'Variations on Common Themes', *New French Feminisms*, ed. E. Marks and I. de Courtivron (Harvester Press, 1977) p. 219.
23. Jacobus, 'The Question of Language: Men of Maxims and the Mill on the Floss', *Critical Inquiry*, vol. 8, no. 2, 'Writing and Difference', 1981, p. 207.
24. Delphy, op. cit.
25. Diana Leonard, 'Male Feminists and Divided Women', in *On the Problem of Men*, ed. S. Friedman and E. Sarah (Women's Press, 1982) p. 161.

CHAPTER 8: BEYOND ALIENATION

1. E. Marks and de I. Courtivron, *New French Feminisms* (Harvester Press, 1981) p. 30.
2. R. Coward, S. Lipshitz and E. Cowie, 'Psychoanalysis and patriarchal structures', in *Papers on Patriarchy*, Women's Publishing Collective (PDC, 1978).
3. Dalston Study Group, 'Was the patriarchy conference "patriarchal"?', in *Papers on Patriarchy*, p. 76.
4. Ibid., p. 77.
5. Simone de Beauvoir, *Memoirs of a Dutiful Daughter*, trans. Kirkup (Penguin 1963) p. 17.

6. Ibid.
7. Roy Harris, *The Language Myth*, (Duckworth, 1981) pp. 87–8.
8. Ibid. pp. 88–9.
9. Ibid., p. 165.
10. Ibid.
11. Beauvoir, op. cit., p. 17.
12. Camilla Gugenheim, 'Man Made Language?' *Amazon*, no. 4, 1981.
13. Audre Lorde, *The Cancer Journals*, (Spinsters Ink, 1980) p. 19.
14. Genesis, 11: 6–9.
15. Trever Pateman, *Language, Truth and Politics*, 2nd edn (Jean Stroud, 1980) p. 129.
16. Cora Kaplan, 'Language and Gender', *Papers on Patriarchy* (WPC/PDC, 1976).
17. Ibid., p. 21.
18. John Oxenham, *Literacy: Writing, Reading and Social Organisation* (Routledge & Kegan Paul, 1980) p. 3.
19. Walter J. Ong, *Orality and Literacy* (Methuen, 1982) p. 113.
20. Oxenham, op. cit., p. 51.
21. Ong, op. cit., p. 3.
22. J. Gumperz, *Discourse Strategies* (CUP, 1982) and J. Gumperz (ed.), *Language and Social Identity* (CUP, 1982).
23. Gumperz, op. cit., pp. 4–5.
24. D. Maltz and R. Borker, 'A Cultural Perspective on Male/Female Miscommunication', in Gumperz, op. cit.
25. Colin McCabe, 'The Discursive and the Ideological in Film', *Screen*, 19/4.
26. M. Black and R. Coward, 'Linguistic, Social and Sexual Relations', *Screen Education*, 39, p. 78.
27. M. Jenkins and C. Kramarae 'A Thief in the House', in *Men's Studies Modified*, ed. Spender (Pergamon, 1981).
28. Kaplan, op. cit., p. 21.
29. Shirley Ardener, *Perceiving Women* (John Wiley, 1975); Philip Smith, 'Sex Markers in Speech', in *Social Markers in Speech*, ed. K. Scherer and H. Giles (CUP, 1979).
30. Marielouise Janssen-Jurreit, *Sexism* (Pluto Press, 1982) p. 284.
31. O. Jespersen, *Language: Its Nature, Development and Origin* (Allen & Unwin, 1922), p. 246.
32. Elinot Keenan, 'Norm Markers, Norm Breakers' in *Explorations in the Ethnography of Speaking*, ed. R. Bauman and J. Sherzer, (CUP, 1974).
33. E. Marks and I. de Courtivron (eds), *New French Feminisms*, p. 5.
34. J.-J. Rousseau, *Emile*, quoted in J. O'Faolain and L. Martines, *Not in God's Image*, (Fontana, 1974) p. 259.
35. Dale Spender, *Man Made Language* (Routledge & Kegan Paul, 1980) p. 107.
36. Cf. Jenkins and Kramarae, op. cit., pp. 16–17.

37. See M. Jenkins and C. Kramer, 'Small group process: learning from women', *WSIQ*, 3, 1980', D. Jones, 'Gossip: notes on women's oral culture', *WSIQ*, 3, 1980.
38. Basil Bernstein, *Class, Codes and Control*, vol. 1, (Routledge & Kegan Paul, 1970).
39. W. Labov, *The Logic of Non-Standard English*, repr. in Giglioli, P. P. (ed.), *Language and Social Context* (Penguin, 1972).
40. Jespersen, *Language*, ch. 24.
41. Dalston Study Group, 'Was the patriarchy conference "patriarchal"?', *Papers on Patriarchy*, p. 77.

CHAPTER 9: CONCLUSION

1. Cheris Kramarae, *Women and Men Speaking* (Newbury House, 1981).
2. Dale Spender, *Man Made Language* (Routledge & Kegan Paul, 1980).
3. Suzette Haden Elgin, Review of *Women and Men Speaking, Language* 58, 1982.
4. Mary Daly, *Gyn/Ecology* (Women's Press, 1978) p. 3.
5. Jean Bethke Elshtain, 'Feminist Discourse and its Discontents', *Feminist Theory*, ed. N. O. Keohane, M. Z. Rosaldo and B. C. Gelpi (Harvester Press, 1982) p. 128.
6. Haden Elgin, op. cit.
7. Trevor Pateman, *Language Truth and Politics* (Jean Stroud, 1980) p. 77.
8. Ibid., pp. 15–16.
9. Ibid., p. 16.
10. Bethke Elshtain, op. cit., p. 129.

Bibliography

Ardener, Edwin, 'Belief and the Problem of Women,' in *Perceiving Women*, ed. S. Ardener (Dent, 1975).

Ardener, Shirley (ed.), *Perceiving Women* (Dent, 1975).

——, *Defining Females* (John Wiley, 1978).

Bales, R. F., 'How People Interact at Conferences', *Communication in Face to Face Interaction*, ed. Laver and Hutcheson (Penguin, 1972).

Barthes, Roland, *Mythologies* (Editions du Seuil, 1957).

Beauvoir, Simone de, *Memoirs of a Dutiful Daughter*, trans. Kirkup (Penguin, 1963).

——, *The Second Sex*, trans. Parshley (Vintage, 1974).

Bernstein, Basil, *Class, Codes and Control, vol. I: Theoretical Studies Towards a Sociology of Language* (Routledge & Kegan Paul, 1970).

Black, Maria and Rosalind Coward, 'Linguistic, Social and Sexual Relations', *Screen Education*, 39, 1981.

Bodine, Ann, 'Androcentrism in Prescriptive Grammar', *Language in Society*, 4, 1975.

Carroll, J. B., *Language, Thought and Reality: Selected Writings of Benjamin Lee Whorf* (MIT Press, 1976).

Chomsky, Noam, review of Skinner's *Verbal Behavior, Language*, 35, 1959.

Cixous, Hélène, 'Sorties', trans. Liddle, *New French Feminisms*, ed. E. Marks and L. de Courtivron (Harvester Press, 1981).

Corbett, Anne, 'Cherchez la metaphor', *Guardian*, 18 Feb. 1983.

Coward, Rosalind and John Ellis, *Language and Materialism* (Routledge and Kegan Paul, 1977).

Coward, Rosalind, Sue Lipshitz and Elizabeth Cowie, 'Psychoanalysis and Patriarchal Structures', in *Papers on Patriarchy* (Women's Publishing Collective/PDC, 1978).

Crystal, David and Derek Davy, *Advanced Conversational English* (Longman, 1975).

Dalston Study Group, 'Was the Patriarchy Conference "Patriarchal"?', *Papers on Patriarchy* (Women's Publishing Collective/PDC, 1978).

Daly, Mary, *Gyn/Ecology: the Metaethics of Radical Feminism* (Women's Press, 1978).

Delphy, Christine, 'A Materialist Feminism is Possible', *Feminist Review*, 4, 1980.

——, 'Women in Stratification Studies', in *Doing Feminist Research*, ed. Helen Roberts (Routledge & Kegan Paul, 1981).

Dubois, Betty Lou and Isobel Crouch, 'The Question of Tag-Questions in Women's Speech; They Don't Really Use More of Them, Do They?' *Language in Society*, 4, 1976.

——, 'American minority women in sociolinguistic perspective', *IJSL* 1978.

Dworkin, Andrea, *Pornography: Men Possessing Women* (Women's Press, 1981).

Elgin, Suzette Haden, review of Kramarae, *Women and Men Speaking*, *Language*, 58, 1982.

Elshtain, Jean Bethke, 'Feminist Discourse and Its Discontents', *Feminist Theory: A Critique of Ideology*, ed. Keohane, Rosaldo and Gelpi (Harvester Press, 1982).

Friedan, Betty, *The Feminine Mystique* (Gollancz, 1963).

Gallop, Jane, 'Psychoanalysis in France', *Women and Literature*, vol. 7, no. 1, 1979.

Grice, H. P., 'Logic in Conversation', *Syntax and Semantics*, vol. III: *Speech Acts*, ed. Cole and Morgan (Academic Press, 1975).

Griffiths, Ian, 'Speech, Writing and Rewriting', unpublished paper, 1982.

Gugenheim, Camilla, 'Man Made Language?' *Amazon*, 4, 1981.

Gumperz, John J. (ed.), *Discourse Strategies* (CUP, 1982).

——, *Language and Social Identity* (CUP, 1982).

Hall, John, *The Sociology of Literature* (Longman, 1979).

Harris, Roy, *The Language Myth* (Duckworth, 1981).

Henton, Caroline, 'Sex Specific Phonetics', unpublished paper, 1983.

Irigaray, Luce, 'Women's Exile' (interview with Couze Venn), *Ideology and Consciousness*, 1, 1977.

——, *Ce Sexe qui n'en est pan un* (Editions Minuit, 1977).

Jacobus, Mary, 'The Question of Language: Men of Maxims and the Mill on the Floss', *Critical Inquiry*, vol. 8, no. 2, 'Writing and difference', 1981.

Janssen-Jurreit, Marielouise, *Sexism: the Male Monopoly of History and Thought* (Pluto Press, 1982).

Jenkins, Mercilee and Cheris Kramarae, 'A Thief in the House: the Case of Women and Language', *Men's Studies Modified*, ed. Spender (Pergamon Press, 1981).

Jespersen, Otto, *Language: Its Nature, Development and Origin* (Allen & Unwin, 1922).

Jones, Deborah, 'Gossip: Notes on Women's Oral Culture', *WSIQ*, 3, 1980.

Kanfer, Stephen, 'Sispeak', *Time*, 23 Oct. 1972.

Kaplan, Cora, 'Language and Gender', *Papers on Patriarchy* (Women's Publishing Collective/PDC, 1978).

Keenan, Elinor O., 'Norm-Makers, Norm-Breakers: Uses of Speech by Women in a Malagasy Community', in *Explorations in the Ethnography of Speaking*, ed. Bauman and Sherzer (CUP, 1974).

Kramarae, Cheris, *Women and Men Speaking* (Newbury House, 1981).

Kristeva, Julia, 'Woman Can Never Be Defined' (interview with psych et po), trans. August, *New French Feminisms*, ed. E. Marks and I. de Courtivron (Harvester Press, 1981).

——, 'Women's time', trans. Jardine and Blake, *Feminist Theory: a Critique of Ideology* ed. Keohane, Rosaldo and Gelpi (Harvester Press, 1982).

Labov, William, *Sociolinguistic Patterns* (University of Pennsylvania Press, 1972).

Lacan, Jacques, *Le Seminaire XX: Encore* (Editions du Seuil, 1975).

Lakoff, Robin, *Language and Woman's Place* (Harper & Row, 1975).

Leonard, Diana, 'Male Feminists and Divided Women', *On the problem of Men*, ed. Friedman and Sarah (Women's Press, 1982).

Lorde, Audre, *The Cancer Journals* (Spinsters Ink, 1980).

Lyons, John, *Introduction to Theoretical Linguistics* (CUP, 1968).

——, (ed.), *New Horizons in Linguistics* (Penguin, 1970).

MacCabe, Colin, 'The Discursive and the Ideological in Film', *Screen*, 19 Apr. 1978.

Maltz, Daniel and Ruth Borker, 'A Cultural Approach to Male/Female Miscommunication', in *Language and Social Identity*, ed. J. Gumperz (CUP, 1982).

Mandelbaum, D., *Selected Writings of Edward Sapir* (University of California Press, 1949).

Marks, Elaine and Isabelle de Courtivron (eds), *New French Feminisms* (Harvester Press, 1981).

Miller, Casey and Kate Swift, *Words and Women: New Language in New Times* (Penguin, 1976).

——, *The Handbook of Non-Sexist Writing* (Women's Press, 1980).

Mitchell, Juliet and Jacqueline Rose (eds). *Feminine Sexuality: Lacan and the École Freudienne* (Macmillan Press, 1982).

Moi, Toril, 'Who's Afraid of Virginia Woolf?, Feminist readings of Woolf' (unpubl. 1982).

——, 'Femininity, Language, Revolution: Julia Kristeva and Anglo-American Feminist Linguistics' (unpublished lecture, 1983). (This paper will form part of Toril Moi's forthcoming book in the New Accents series published by Methuen on Feminist Criticism.)

O'Faolain, Julia and Lauro Martines, *Not in God's Image* (Fontana, 1974).

Ong, Walter J, *Orality and Literacy: The Technologizing of the Word* (Methuen, 1982).

Orwell, George, 'Politics and the English Language,' *Collected Essays* (Secker & Warburg, 1961).

Oxenham, John, *Literacy: Writing, Reading & Social Organisation* (Routledge & Kegan Paul, 1980).

Pateman, Trevor, *Language, Truth and Politics: Towards a Radical Theory for Communication*, 2nd edn (Jean Stroud, 1980).

Pellowe, John, G. Nixon, B. Strang and V. McNeany, 'A Dynamic Modelling of Lingusitic Variation: the Urban (Tyneside) Linguistic Survey', *Lingua*, 30, 1972.

Rich, Adrienne, *On Lies, Secrets and Silence: Selected Prose 1966–78* (Virago, 1980).

Saussure, Ferdinand de, *Course in General Linguistics*, trans. Baskin (Fontana, 1974).

Scherer, Klaus and Howard Giles (eds), *Social Markers in Speech* (CUP, 1979).

Schulz, Muriel, 'The Semantic Derogation of Women', *Language and Sex: Difference and Dominance*, ed. Thorne and Henley (Newbury House, 1975).

Scruton, Roger, 'How Newspeak Leaves Us Naked', *The Times*, 1 Feb 1983.

Smith, Dorothy, 'A Peculiar Eclipsing! Women's Exclusion from Men's Culture', *WSIQ* 1, 1978.

Smith, Philip M., 'Sex Markers in Speech', *Social Markers in Speech*, ed. Scherer and Giles (CUP, 1979) ch. 6.

Spender, Dale, *Man Made Language* (Routledge & Kegan Paul, 1980).

Swift, Jonathan, 'A Proposal for Correcting the English Tongue', *Prose Works of Jonathan Swift*, Vol. IV, ed. H. Davis (Blackwell, 1957).

Trudgill, Peter, 'Sex, Covert Prestige and Linguistic Change in the Urban British English of Norwich', *Language in Society*, 1, 1972.

Zimmerman, Don and Candace West, 'Sex Roles, Interruptions and Silences in Conversation', in *Language and Sex: Difference and Dominance*', ed. Thorne and Henley (Newbury House, 1975).

Glossary

ACCENT pronunciation.

ACCOMMODATION unconscious process by which speaker modifies her speech to be more like the person she is talking to.

ALIENATION in feminist linguistic theories, a term used for the inability to express your own experience because no suitable framework/vocabulary exists. Also a technical term in marxist writing.

APHASIA speech impairment or loss caused by damage to the left side of the brain.

BACK CHANNELING giving a speaker cues such as 'yes', 'mhm', etc.

BEHAVIOURISM an approach to psychology that studies only observable behaviour and not consciousness or mental states. Associated with 'stimulus response' explanations of activity (i.e. particular actions are responses to specific stimuli) and conditioning techniques (i.e. training animals to perform tasks by rewarding and punishing them). Behaviorism was popular with later American structuralist linguists, and the leading figure in opposing it was the linguist Chomsky.

BIOLOGISM the tendency to explain things by reducing them to biological causes – e.g. 'anatomy is destiny'.

CODE SWITCHING changing from one language or variety to another according to the subject or the situation of talk.

COMPETENCE Chomsky's term for the knowledge of grammatical rules the native speaker has internalised: opposed to **PERFORMANCE**, the use she makes of the rules.

COMPONENTIAL ANALYSIS approach to breaking down word-meanings. Words are given plus or minus values on a number of 'primitive' semantic features such as 'animate', 'human', etc.

CONJOINING linguist's term for making complex sentences using conjunctions like **AND** and **BUT**.

CORPUS the finite speech sample a linguist works on. General linguists gave up corpus analysis after the 'Chomsky revolution' but sociolinguists, discourse analysts, phoneticians and psycholinguists still make use of corpora either 'natural' (surreptitiously recorded) or (more often) deliberately elicited under laboratory or other formal conditions.

COVERT PRESTIGE the value certain groups attach to non-standard dialect features. Proposed by Trudgill as an explanation of why men deviate more than women from standard norms.

DECONSTRUCTION a reading process associated with post-structuralism in which the aim is to expose contradictions and lacunae in a text.

DEMOGRAPHIC VARIABLE something that varies in the population (i.e. from speaker to speaker according to social categories like age, class, race and sex) and not according to the type and formality of the situation.

DETERMINISM in linguistics, the belief that linguistic structures are ultimately responsible for their users' conceptualisation of the physical and intellectual universe. Associated with Sapir and Whorf, and also latterly with Saussure.

DIACHRONIC historical.

DIALECT cluster of lexical, grammatical and phonological features associated with a particular regional or social group.

DIALECTOLOGY literally, the study of dialects; more usually, the historical analysis of rural language varieties, opposed to 'urban dialectology' which is more usually called *sociolinguistics*.

DISCOURSE in linguistics, language 'above the level of the sentence', i.e. exchanges in talk; in semiology, a set of related utterances. (Linguists define discourse syntagmatically, whereas for semiologists discourses are paradigmatic phenomena.)

EMBEDDING making complex sentences by using what are traditionally called subordinate clauses (e.g. that fish *I bought yesterday* was off) where the italicised section is embedded.

EMPIRICISM is science, a methodology which tests hypotheses by experiment or observation: characterised by the use of evidence to support theory. In philosophy, the belief that there are no innate ideas, and all knowledge derives from experience.

ESSENTIALISM the belief that your object of study has certain basic qualities which do not need to be explained; they themselves will do as an explanation of other qualities. An example is 'human nature' as an explanation of human behaviour. One important characteristic of most semiology is its implacable opposition to all essentialist statements.

ETYMOLOGY the study of the history and derivation of words.

FERAL wild. Used of children who grow up outside human society.

FOLKLINGUISTICS linguist's term for the beliefs of non-linguists about language.

FORMALISM a preoccupation with the way statements are expressed; often prescribes a standard notation or terminology.

GENDER in grammar, a property of nouns with requires adjectives and pronouns to agree with it. In feminist theory generally, socially constructed male/femaleness as opposed to biological male/femaleness which is called **SEX**.

GRAMMAR   the practice of linguists; the model made by linguists; the level of language between sound and meaning, i.e. form-morphology and syntax; rules for correct usage (prescriptive grammar).

GUTTURAL   made at the back of the vocal tract. Linguists no longer use this term, which has become a folklinguistic insult for Germans, Geordies, etc. lacking its original technical meaning.

IDEALISATION   modification of raw data (usually by ignoring some of it and treating the rest selectively) to make it more manageable or regular. In linguistics the point of idealisation is normally the exclusion of extra-linguistic context and 'insignificant' variation.

INDETERMINACY   inability to be stated definitively.

INFORMANT   linguist's term for the person who produces her corpus or takes part in her experiment.

INFORMATION THEORY   study of message-transmission, efficiency and processing.

INTONATION   use of pitch contrasts in speech: gives grammatical and attitudinal information.

LANGUE   Saussure's term for the linguistic system which makes possible individual speech acts (*PAROLE*).

LEXICOGRAPHY   dictionary-making.

LOGOCENTRISM   primacy of the (written) word; the term is popular with post-structuralist followers of Jacques Derrida.

MARKING THEORY   theory that linguistic elements form pairs or sets that are hierarchically ordered, one being more neutral (and thus frequent) than the other(s).

MATERIALISM   the philosophy associated with marxism. Rejects explanations based on ideas or supernatural concepts.

METALINGUISTIC   about or beyond language. Used in this book with broader reference than in most linguistics texts, which confine the term to a particular set of *words* (i.e. those used by expert and lay speakers to talk about language, like *noun* or *meaning*). I use it also to describe practices and institutions that are parasitic on language, such as grammar, dictionaries, etc.

METHODOLOGY   the principles and techniques of scientific research. Increasingly synonymous with **METHOD** but used in scientific or pseudo-scientific registers.

MORPHOLOGY   internal structure of words.

NON-STANDARD   variety of language which lacks prestige or is not officially sanctioned. Typically a non-standard has no writing system, is not widely diffused and is spoken by the least educated and poorest members of a society.

PEJORATION   word used for the process by which something (e.g. a word) comes to have negative connotations.

PERFORMANCE   language use: see **COMPETENCE**.

PHILOLOGY   the historical study of linguistic texts.

PHONETICS   study of speech sounds.

PHONOLOGY   study of sound systems, i.e. how speech sounds are deployed meaningfully in languages.

POSITIVISM   philosophy of science dominant in 19th and 20th centuries.

POST-STRUCTURALISM   development in philosophy and criticism associated with Derrida, so-called because it came after the structuralism of theorists like Lévi-Strauss and Barthes. The 'technique' of post-structuralism is **deconstruction**.

PRESCRIPTIVISM   the use of value-judgements and notions of correctness in grammar.

PROSODY   in speech, intonation, stress and rhythm; in verse, metre.

REFERENT   what in the real world a word refers to.

REGISTER   variety of language appropriate in content, medium (speech/writing/whistling/drumming/signing), style and tone to its particular domain of use.

REIFICATION   treating a concept as a thing.

RELATIVITY   the notion that different cultures classify reality differently (therefore that it is effectively a different reality depending on who's interpreting it). Linguistic relativity is the theory associated with Sapir and (especially) Whorf (see **DETERMINISM**).

SEMANTICS   study of meaning.

SEMIOLOGY   science of signs based on Saussurean principles. Used particularly for 'theory of the subject', i.e. Lacanian influenced theory, but also for structuralist and post-structuralist film and literary criticism, etc.

SIGN   the unit of language according to Saussure, consisting of a signifier (form) and a signified (concept) indissolubly joined together, and deriving its significance from a contrast with other such signs rather from its own substance, which is arbitrary.

SOCIAL MARKER   linguistic feature associated with a particular demographic or situational variable.

SOCIOBIOLOGY   also called 'selfish gene theory': a biologistic explanation of human behaviour and human social structures.

SPEECH COMMUNITY   an idealisation; the term refers to any group of people sharing the same linguistic norms, but isolating such a group in practice is quite impossible.

STANDARD   the officially sanctioned or most prestigious language variety within a state.

STEREOTYPE   in linguistics, a folklinguistic characterisation of some group's speech.

STRATIFICATION particular statistical pattern; in sociolinguistics it is produced by dividing a sample according to socioeconomic class and quantifying each group's use of certain stereotypical linguistic features.

STRUCTURALISM methodology based on Saussurean principle that systems are sets of differences. In Linguistics, refers to the American movement of Bloomfield, Hockett, *et al.*; in general, refers to the French theorists Lévi-Strauss, Barthes, etc.

STYLE variety of language associated with situational features, particularly formality as perceived by the participants.

STYLE SHIFT moving from one style to another as you perceive increased/decreased formality.

STYLISTICS the study of style and register, and especially of literary uses of language.

SYNCHRONIC not historical.

SYNTAGMATIC relationship of elements that can be combined. Opposed to **PARADIGMATIC** or **ASSOCIATIVE** relationships, in which the related elements can substitute for one another in the same context.

SYNTAX the study of sentence structure.

TRANSFORMATIONAL GRAMMAR Chomsky's theory of language. The name derives from a new sort of rule (a 'transformation') which was central to the model. TG is distinguished by its formalism, mentalism and commitment to universals.

UNIVERSAL in linguistics, a feature or tendency common to all languages.

VARIATION the heterogeneity typical in linguistic data.

VARIETY neutral term for any kind of language (i.e. dialect, style, register, etc.).

VERNACULAR historically, a mother-tongue (as opposed to learned languages such as Latin, which were the vehicle of culture and scholarship but had to be learned at school, after first-language acquisition). In sociolinguistics, the style furthest from prestige norms, used in casual situations when monitoring is minimal and therefore of great theoretical interest to the linguist.

Index